Forward

I believe we are living in the most ͟ though they may not be easiest of days. History is being made like never before. I also believe that mindfulness is going to be imperative to our well being in the turbulent times ahead. Since 2020 the world has been in a state of anxiety and chaos, I have met a lot of people who have been adversely affected emotionally, spiritually and physically.

It would appear we still have rocky times ahead which will add to the instability many have already experienced. But, if we can stay centred and mindful we can come out the other side of this experience stronger than ever and we might even enjoy the ride.

Living in a mindful way is not difficult, it just requires practice and for us to be kind and patient with ourselves. Every moment is an opportunity to enrich our lives through mindfulness.

Love the experience, grow stronger

MINDFULNESS FOR LIVING

BY
ELIZABETH R

Copyright 2023 by Elizabeth R Gelhard
All rights reserved. No part of this book may be reproduced, transmitted, or stored in any form or by means, whether written, printed, electronic or otherwise without the prior permission of :
Elizabeth R Gelhard

ERG.UK@outlook.com

Book and cover design by Elizabeth R Gelhard

© Elizabeth R Gelhard 2023

Dedication

I would like to dedicate this book to my beautiful grandson Koby. My little guru, with each year he grows a little wiser, and brings much love and joy.

Forward
Dedication
Introduction
(No mountain, no mist, no rainbows or unicorns)
1 WHAT IS MINDFULNESS?
2 COMING TO OUR SENSES
3 EMOTIONS
4 MIND WHAT YOU ARE   EATING
5 OBSERVING THE NATURAL WORLD
6 JUST SITTING
7 MINDFUL MEDITATION
8 HOBBIES
9 SLEEP
10 CRYSTALS
11 MINDFUL COMMUNICATION
12 MINDFULNESS IN DIFFICULT TIMES
13 LOST DOWN THE TECHNICAL RABBIT HOLE
14 THANK YOU WORLD, UNIVERSE,
ANGELS, GOD - or whatever you believe in
15 THE JOY OF LIFE
16 THE MUNDANE - Opportunity for mindfulness
17 HEALTH BENEFITS OF MINDFULNESS

Introduction
(No mountain, no mist, no rainbows or unicorns)

How often have you heard that practising mindfulness is good for our mental wellbeing? Magazines are full of articles explaining the benefits of mindfulness. Unfortunately, they do not always tell us how to become mindful. So you might wonder how do we 'do it' Do we need to find a guru, a teacher?

Actually I did find a teacher, I want to tell you about my teacher and what he taught me. What image forms in your mind when I say I found a guru/teacher? Do you think of a bearded, wise, old man sitting on a mountain, shrouded in a mist of transcendental dreaminess? This is the vision many people get when they hear the term 'mindfulness guru'. If there is such a guru sitting on said mountain then that mental image is correct. However, my teacher came in the shape of a chubby toddler, babbling happily at his own fingers and toes.

Allow me introduce you to a very wise, tiny child who has prompted me to explore mindfulness and enrich my life in ways I would not have considered, had it not been for his teachings.

Let me share with you what I have learnt and introduce you to practical easy ways of being mindful in daily life. By which, I mean hard core, feet on the ground mindfulness. Mindfulness is not about being in a state of dreamy Lala land all rainbows and unicorns.

Mindfulness is about being total alert. Alert to ourselves and alert to our environment and what is occurring around us. When we are mindful, we are out of our headspace and fully present and conscious in the world which we are meant to inhabit. When we are mindful we are wide awake. When we are mindful we are not only alive but we are living in the here and now.
When we are *not* mindful we are often dreaming a nightmare of thought.

Despite the lack of magical mountains, rainbows and unicorns if we practice mindfulness, we can feel much more peaceful, calm and loving. Actually, there can be rainbows and magical mountains but you must find them yourself. The important thing to remember is that you can derive much more pleasure from them than you would if you were not being mindful.

I am extremely blessed because I am a grandmother to a lovely boy. It was through observing my little grandson, my tiny guru, that I became aware, of his total immersion in the business of experiencing life. As a therapist I had spent many years practising meditation and mindfulness, however, it gradually became apparent to me that he was the living epitome of mindfulness and that he had a lot to teach me.

Tiny children can help us to remember who and what we are, and where we are. Whenever I had the opportunity, I observed my tiny guru and I considered how I could incorporate his demonstration of living in a mindful manner into my own life and my way of being. To enter into the world that children inhabit, is to remember the magic of life.

The aim of this book is to share with you some of what I have learnt so far from my tiny guru alongside some of the practices which I have found work for me and my clients. And to suggest ways in which you might incorporate mindfulness into your daily activities. I want to invite you to experience how easy it is, with just a little practice, to weave mindfulness into daily living. You will be amazed at how much more of an enriched life you can live by being totally connected to the here and now.

It is my opinion that mindfulness should not be something we enter into for just 20 minutes each day as part of a spiritual ritual such as meditation. I believe that daily meditation is life enriching but it is just a one possible piece, of the beautiful mosaic, of a glorious life.

There is a whole industry built around teaching us how to be mindful even though, it is something which at a basic level should, be as natural to us as breathing.

Unfortunately, due to the technological age we are currently living in and our thirst for continuous achievement at an ever increasingly rapid rate of momentum, many of us have lost touch with both ourselves and the wonderful physical world around us. As we dive ever deeper into the cyber world, we forget more and more who, what and where we are, and we loose the opportunity of truly experiencing being alive. Nowadays, we see people walking up a high street with their eyes glued to their mobile telephones even worse people ignoring the laws not to mention common sense using their text app whilst driving!

We see people in restaurants in conversation with social media 'friends' and totally ignoring the real people sat at the same dining table. Some people appear to get more enjoyment out of photographing their meal than they do from actually eating it. I always feel very sad when I see couples on their mobile devices ignoring their children.

The messages these adults are giving those children are in my opinion not good. I am sure that they are loving parents in many ways. But, they are not teaching the children how to communicate face to face. Instead, they are telling their children that they are less important and less worthy of attention than a small screen.

It is not possible to be reading a screen and fully in touch with the here and now. Or in other words we can either put our attention in the cyber world or we can focus our awareness on the moment we are supposed to be living in the physical world. No matter what we tell ourselves it is really not possible to do both.

We are told that the eyes are the window to the soul, so maybe we need to look into people's eyes and connect with their soul and not make a piece of plastic in our hands more important than the toddler in the high chair. And let us not forget do not forget that, that tiny tot in the high chair has much to teach us.

Small children do not need to be told to be mindful, it is natural for them to touch, feel, look at the world around them and to feel part of everything. I have had the honour of being taught by a small child how to re-connect with this wonderful world. I feel it is now my job to ensure that my tiny guru (who is not so tiny anymore) doesn't forget what he has taught me. We often have discussions about the on-line games he likes to play with his friends and how that world is different from the 'real' world. As devices such as virtual reality headsets become more popular the lines become more blurred. I am not against technology including AI but when we allow it to take over huge chunks of our lives mindfulness slips away from us.

Mindfulness is often seen as a spiritual practice and indeed it can certainly help those of us who choose to focus on the spiritual journey in order to develop our consciousness. But mindfulness can also be an aid to enrich the lives of those who have no interest in what they view as 'spiritual matters'.

I would argue that, people lived mindful lives well before the phrase was coined. Ancient peoples were aware of the world around them and their place in it, long before the Lord Buddha brought forth his teachings.

In this modern world I can work in my garden and at the same time listen to music or an on-line discussion, I can weed the garden and at the same time educate myself on world events. All of which may have great benefits. But, it takes away my concentration from the job in hand, the feeling of working with nature, the very essence of nurturing the plants that will in time bring joy from their colours and perfumes or in the case of edibles will feed me and my family.

Past generations were immersed in the tasks they undertook. Nowadays, we need to remind ourselves often enough to be mindful until mindfulness becomes second nature once again. I hope this book will encourage you to do so.

Mindfulness is often associated with Buddhism. I believe that it is true that buddhists do use mindfulness as a huge part of their spiritual practice. In order to change their sense of self and their perception of the world . However, I am not aiming to share buddhist teachings, this book is written from a totally secular point of view. I do not wish to offend people by saying mindfulness can be taken away from any particular belief system. I know that some people will disagree with me because humans like to have ownership of ideas, this despite the fact that, many people can have the same basic beliefs without a religious or political tag.

I think it is fair to point out that people all over the world, from various backgrounds and belief systems have used the same or, broadly similar strategies and practices to those I am offering in this book. I am pretty sure that our ancestors were very much living in the present moment when they were hunting on the Great plains, fishing in the North Sea or trekking through dense jungle. Or any other activity that involved being aware of their actions and their interaction with the natural environment around them.

Today, if we are involved in sports, mountaineering/climbing, or administering surgery or driving through busy city traffic we have to be in the same state of awareness as our ancestors were. Nonetheless, I believe that whilst we are often carrying out daily activities which require less concentration than let us say for instance, negotiating tricky terrain on a mountain bike, we are seldom truly immersed in what we are doing or even how we are doing it.

We all know that we should be mindful when driving a vehicle, but I must put my hands up and confess I am not always and I suspect few people are all the time. I hasten to add that although I may not always be mindful when I am driving my car, I am always careful. Being mindful and being careful are not the same. I promise you that I never have and never will drive whilst texting on my mobile telephone but, I may sometimes allow my attention to stray to what I have to do when I arrive at my destination or what is playing on the car radio. In those moments I am not mindful.

Despite the fact that most of us in the Western world have more technology to help us with our daily tasks, life seems to be becoming more and more stressful for a lot of people. If we incorporate mindfulness practices into our daily life it can help us get through stressful times. Which means we are more able to cope with feelings of being under pressure and anxiety, and to some degree it can help us to avoid becoming stressed in the first place.

I have included in this book a lot of practical mindfulness exercises and activities and hope that you enjoy trying them. Please be clear that I am not aiming to give you a written course of what is often referred to as mindfulness cognitive therapy (MCG). MCG is often a group therapy programme lasting for several weeks where mindfulness techniques are blended with cognitive education. Such programmes tend to be designed for the treatment of depression. It is my understanding that Some people who have periods of depression find that the skills learnt on MCG programmes can help them through the depression and prevent future relapses.

If you feel that such therapy would be of benefit to you I would encourage you to explore the subject and to talk to a professional for guidance on the matter.

I sincerely hope that you find this book of interest and that you gain helpful insight into how you can enrich your own life. When we find ways of improving our lives through our own actions we become powerful.

1 WHAT IS MINDFULNESS?

I have touched on it in the introduction but let us explore further. There is a huge array of information and courses available on the subject of mindfulness. I can only give you my take on what being mindful means to me.

Let us start by trying to understand why children are adepts at living a life in a mindful way. I think that it is excellent that in recent years some schools in the UK have started introducing mindfulness to very young children. I believe that if we encourage children from an early age to be mindful and if we continue with that encouragement throughout their learning years, when those children grow up, we will have some much happier and less stressed adults than has been the case in recent years.

It is interesting that we need to teach children how to be mindful considering they demonstrate mindfulness in their early stages of life as a natural state of being. I wonder what happens that they forget to be mindful? Children come into this world equipped to be fully in the present moment but they loose it. This raises the question of, is it nature or nurture that humans move from being fully in touch with their environment and how they feel emotionally, to a state of disassociation from that which is not occupying their thoughts?

We know that children experience the world through the brain state/frequency/wave cycle they are in. Brain waves are the electrical activity occurring in the brain. We have four types of brain wave. The first seven years of a human's life are the programming years which is why the Jesuits maxim is said to have been 'Give me the child until he is seven and I will give you the man'.

For the first two years of their lives children are in the delta wave cycle. This is the state we all, including adults, go into when we have a deep restorative sleep, in delta wave frequency we have very little critical thinking or judgement.

Between the ages of two and six years of age children are, in the theta brain state. They are connected to their own internal world, and they are in the realm of imagination, it is a time when they are open to suggestion and it is a super learning state. This theta frequency is the brain state that those of us who practise hypnosis guide our clients into. Theta is a state of relaxation and is the frequency of REM sleep.

Between the ages of five and eight the child moves into alpha brain wave frequency. This is the analytical mind coming into awareness, however, the inner world of imagination is as real as the outer reality. One could say that they have a foot in both worlds the inner and the outer. When we meditate this is the frequency we tend to enter into.

Around the ages of eight to twelve years the child moves into Beta. Most adults would believe they spend most of their time in Beta. This is conscious, focused, analytical, logical thinking. I believe that we should be offering children the opportunity to learn meditation from about eight years of age but of course it does depend on the child and their receptivity. I believe we should certainly be encouraging them to practice mindfulness.

I have listened to a lot of people talking about mindfulness, I've read books by famous gurus, attended workshops and watched YouTube videos. Yes, I have learnt techniques and helpful exercises from all of these sources of information, however, I can honestly say I have learnt as much from my tiny guru aka my little grandson as I have from all the experts. I invite you to learn from the little ones and also to encourage them to continue to be the beautiful mindful beings they are naturally, so that unlike many of us adults, they don't have to re-learn. I also think we should consider how we teach them something and then we purposefully undo that teaching. For instance we buy or make tactile/sensory toys for them, such toys come in all forms from simple rattles to wooden boards with brightly coloured things that turn and slide and make noises to tubes holding glitter in fluid. We put them into seats surrounded by themed carousels that turn around them making a variety of sounds from animal noises to music. We hang mobiles over the cots. We shake teddies and rattles at them and make crazy sounds for them to copy.

Sometimes it appears to me that they can be sensory overloaded by the non-stop activity and sounds aimed at their little brains. Then, as soon as they are old enough to get out of the baby bouncer and start exploring the world we are constantly telling them 'No' and taking things off them. We don't want them to hurt themselves and we don't want grannies silk blouse spoilt by grubby little hands even if we have previously spent months smiling at them and telling them how clever they are to touch anything that came within reach of their tiny fingers. "Ahh look, he loves his teddy bear, don't you our clever little boy?" we say as he pulls teddy's foot out of his mouth waving it in the air and flicking baby dribble over everything within ten paces. Six months later we snatch grannies furry hat from him just as it is about to get the snot and dribble treatment. And we admonish him for touching it and tell him it's grannies and not his.

We can't wait for little ones to be able to walk and when they do, we try to curb their exploration of the world.

We get very excited at their first words and praise them for making a sound that might sound a little bit like momma or dada but when they get to the stage of talking we tell them to shush when we think they are vocal at inappropriate times.

Then when they are a little older in school we try to teach them mindfulness which is about being in touch with our surroundings, touch, smell, sound, and being non-judgemental. Is it any wonder we have the stage known as 'the terrible twos.'

If you research the meaning of the term mindfulness you will find a variety of descriptors including the following types of explanation

Having awareness of what is going on inside and outside ourselves moment by moment

Noticing what is happening in the present moment in your mind, your body and your surroundings without judgement

Being in a state of conscious awareness of something

Allowing thoughts to arrive without allowing them to control you and your actions

A mental state achieved by focusing one's awareness on the present moment whilst calmly acknowledging and accepting one's own feelings, thoughts, and bodily sensations.

My own definition of mindfulness is - Living in the moment by being fully absorbed in the whole experience of that moment physically, mentally and spiritually and most important of all, loving the feeling of being alive.

Scientific research, tells us that practicing mindfulness can change the way both our bodies and brains work, for the better. Regular practice of mindfulness has the power to: increase activity in the parts of your brain that are involved with all of the following; emotional regulation, learning, memory, perspective and self-talk. It can also help with immune responses, improve sleep and in some cases it can even decrease pain.

The average adult spends most of their time not being in a state of mindfulness. How much time do we spend carrying out a task and at the same time planning what we are going to do next? I think most of us are guilty of this sort of behaviour. For instance, whilst getting ourselves ready to go to work, thinking about what we will do when we arrive at our place of employment. Or thinking about the route we will take to where we are working that day. Another thing we humans do is look back at what we have done, or re-living conversations we have had with someone. I think most of us do this, for example, the morning I wrote this chapter for this book, as I was washing up the breakfast things, I was planning what to cook for lunch! See, even those of us who try to live a life in a state of mindfulness, constantly slip out of that state, but that is okay.

The important thing is to try to observe ourselves behaving in this way without judgement of ourselves. When we learn to observe ourselves, we can bring ourselves back into mindfulness. It is very important that we do not to judge ourselves.

When we focus on thinking we have somehow failed to be mindful we are judging ourselves. When we are judging ourselves we are not in a place of mindfulness because, we are looking back at the past (even if that past is only a few minutes ago) also, by judging ourselves to be 'not good enough' we are allowing negative emotions to take control and of course the whole point of mindfulness is to feel positive about ourselves and our life.

To return to the example washing up the breakfast dishes and thinking about what to cook for the next meal. Had I been in a mindful state, I would have been looking at the objects I was washing, feeling the shape and finish of them, looking at, listening to and feeling the movement of my hands interacting with the water, maybe smelling the detergent, seeing the colours in the bubbles, aware of my body posture and hand movements. I would have been aware of my surroundings in my kitchen which looks out into the garden. I could have been aware of the sunlight through the window, conscious of my own inner state of mind.

As it was, even though my thoughts were elsewhere, subconsciously I would have been aware of all these things, but, not consciousness. In other words not fully engaged in the task.

You might be wondering what was wrong with planning the next meal, the answer to that question is nothing. There is absolutely nothing wrong with planning future actions. We all have to do some planning at some time. If we failed to plan our cupboards would be empty and tasks not completed. But, we can be mindful of the planning process which we are involved in by, observing ourselves and our thoughts.

The mismatch or lack of mindfulness occurs when we go into automatic mode ie carrying out a task without being aware of where our hands are whilst our mind, is elsewhere. In my household there are frequent conversations regarding where keys have been put, both vehicle and house keys. We have a basket where all keys are supposed to be kept when not in use. The reason keys often cannot be located is because, they have been left in pockets, handbags, on dressing tables and sometimes still in the outside door locks. This is because we are not present in the moment and are unaware of what we are doing.

Dropping a key into a pocket or handbag is done on automatic pilot whilst the mind is focused elsewhere. In other words, not being present in the moment. Not being present in the moment of our life, not aware that we are alive. It is very easy to slip from the present 'now moment' into the past or the future. Remember, what has gone has gone and, you cannot change it. But, you can spoil the present moment, by worrying about what has not yet happened in the future, or by getting into a panic because you cannot find your car keys and are going to be late for an appointment. I love the old quote 'Yesterday is history, tomorrow is a mystery, we only have this moment in time which is a gift, that is why we call it the **'present'**.

The more we practice mindfulness the more pleasant and less stressful life becomes. Things, people, situations, unpleasant sights, sounds and thoughts become less upsetting. If we learn to shift our relationship from aversion to curiosity, allowing life to flow and embracing whatever we are involved in things really improve for us. Just by being aware, having a childlike curiosity helps life become fun. This is all mindfulness.

Before we go any further, let us look at what mindfulness is not. Mindfulness is not a faith system, cult, religion or holistic treatment. Mindfulness is not self hypnosis nor is it being empty minded.

Unfortunately, mindfulness is not a magic wand to remove all worries, stress or anxiety. But it can certainly help us live more fully.

Live every moment

2 COMING TO OUR SENSES

Mindfulness is about being fully aware in the present 'now'. We will start exploring mindfulness by looking at some of the components of our awareness navigation system beginning with, our five senses of touch, sight, sound, smell and taste. Let us start to consider how instead of just letting these senses run in the background, we can be fully aware and bring them to the fore so that we can start to really wring as much juice out of life as is possible.

TOUCH

Just like my little grandson did as a tiny tot, I like to feel nice textures. When you go into a shop to purchase clothing, do you choose your purchase just on what the item looks like? Or do you feel the textile the item is made from? I think most people purchase clothing on how it feels, what it feels like to wear, how comfortable it is, also the texture of the fabric. We often think that we can tell the quality of an expensive item by how it feels to the touch. Besides, nobody wants anything scratchy next to their skin do they?

It's not only clothing that we like to feel, curtain samples hung in shops get felt, carpets are patted and hands run over them for softness, as do soft new fluffy towels. The steering wheels in showroom cars get squeezed and fingers arc backwards and forwards feeling their smoothness and grip points. We like to feel with our hands the finish of wooden items such as furniture and carved ornaments.

But, how often do we notice the tactile properties of the items once we have purchased them? When buying cushions we squeeze and pat them, but, once they are in our home, how often do we plump them up and straighten them without hardly noticing the feel of them?

As a child I loved the feeling of pulling on brand new socks and I still do. Something that one can often observe and always makes me smile is what I call 'The Sock Game' which tiny tots play with adults. My tiny guru was an adept at 'The Sock Game.' This game is often played by a child in their baby buggy or pushchair, usually on a sunny day when they are wearing socks but not shoes. Somehow the child wriggles their little toes until they get at least one sock off their foot and onto the floor. The adult replaces the sock often ending with a smile and gentle pat to the sole of the little foot and a short time later it is wriggled off the foot again. If they are an adept at the game, they can sometimes manage to flick it off the foot and over their shoulder or they might get it into their little fist or it may be on the floor. This can go on for quite a while until one of them gives in. In my experience it is usually the adult who concedes first and removes both socks and stuffs them into the bag at the back of the pushchair leaving little toes to wiggle freely in the fresh air. The question I always ask myself is, why does the child remove the sock? Is it because their feet are too warm? Is it because they don't want their toes to be restricted? In which case they are in touch with their physical body. It might be that they enjoy the sensation of the fabric moving over the skin as it is removed and replaced. It might be they just want the adults attention, in which case they want to enjoy the sensation of the verbal, eye and physical contact which means, they are aware of the how such contact feels. At the end of the day the child is using mindful awareness. Most adults don't even feel their feet unless they stub a toe or get a blister on their heel. I know that once my feet are encased in socks or other footwear I am usually absolutely unaware of them

Mindful exercises-touch
Try the following five exercises as you go through your day.

1. The next time that someone you love, embraces you, really absorb the feeling and become that hug.

2. Unless our attention is drawn to it, once we get into the business of the day, most of us have no awareness of the clothing we are wearing. We might notice if something is uncomfortable or if we feel to hot or too cold and need to

change or moderate what we are wearing by removing or adding a layer.

Right now, as you read this, try to be aware of the clothing that you are wearing, not by looking at it but have an awareness of it touching your skin, run your hands down a sleeve or leg .

When you get dressed look at each item before you put it on, feel the texture, be aware of the thickness of the fabric, notice the weight of it in your hands does it smell new or of laundry products? When you put it on, be aware of it in your hands, feel it touching the skin as it passes over before being in place. When it is in place, take notice of how it feels. Be aware of you in that piece of apparel, how do you feel?

3. The next time you get yourself a clean towel from your cupboard, shelf or wherever you store your towels. Look at it as if it was something new that you were consider purchasing, feel it. Notice the thickness of the pile, the closeness of the weave, how soft is it? Does it have a pleasant smell to it? When you dry your hands or body what does that feel like?

4. Hold any (non sharp) everyday object in your hand, close your eyes and feel it. Feel it's texture, it's warmth or coolness, move it around in your hand so you hold it from every angle. You might find that an object you see daily but don't really look at becomes a new object when experienced purely through

touch. Ask yourself if you feel a different connection to the object when you experience it through touch alone. Then experience the same object using all of your senses. Is there a difference?

5. As you go through your day, try to be more aware of the surfaces and objects you are touching.

SIGHT

Although we see things as we move around in our environment, a lot of the time we do not see with awareness. This is not surprising, as it is believed, that the human brain processes billions of bits of information every second, we are however only conscious of a couple of thousand of those bits of information.

We are being bombarded with more and more material not only from our immediate surroundings, but also, as we take on an increasing amount of data from the media and especially the internet. Not only are world and his wife constantly clamouring for our attention, because of the tumultuous times we are living through, many of us are continually, actively looking for information in order to keep abreast of changing situations. I believe that it is very easy for us as individual entities to become sucked up and lost in a tumultuous sea of sensory overload which, can be very stressful to the human nervous system. For this reason, bringing ourselves back to mindful awareness is a useful tool for restoring us into balance.

Those of us who have visual sight, experience huge parts of our lives through what we see including; our homes, the smiles and other facial expressions of those we love and of course other people's body language, which is understood to be a huge part of human communication. Our sight helps us to manoeuvre ourselves around the world with a good degree of safety so that we avoid tripping up steps, grabbing sharp knives or walking off cliff tops. Our eyes allow us to see words in a book or on a screen, the food we eat, the natural world around us, our children and grandchildren's first steps.

I can remember the first time my newborn grandson looked at me, we locked eyes and I felt that we knew each other at a deep soul level. At that moment I fell in love. Exactly the same thing happened with my daughter when she was a newborn. It has been said many times that the eyes are the window to the soul, in which case one could argue that it is the soul that looks out of those windows therefore, surely we should nourish our souls with what we focus our eyes on, including, the information we consume from the media. I do not mean just what is fed to us as 'the news' but also films and videos etc. No matter where we look at them, be that on the television, newspapers, cinema or internet. There have been debates for many years regarding how violent films even cartoons can have a negative affect on children. I have often wondered why the same debate doesn't take place regarding what adults consume in the name of entertainment.

In almost all of the exercises in this book you are encouraged if you are able to, to look at things visually. Really looking at objects and engaging with them is very different to glancing at something. It is impossible for the human brain to have conscious awareness of every detail that comes into our field of vision. We cannot register at a glance every line on the palm of our hands as individual pieces of information, but we can focus on each of those individual lines. Likewise we cannot register every blade of grass in a lawn, or every detail in a room but we can bring our focus to elements of such scenes which gives us an overall view. The following is a very simple exercise. How much time you spend on these practices is up to you and will of course be dependent on how much time you have and how comfortable you feel with the process.

Mindful exercise - sight
Find a place where you can view an outside scene. If you are able to sit on a bench or a wall besides a road or in a park

do so, otherwise, sit besides a window where you can view the outside world.

Try to observe all you see without being critical of anything, remember that suspending judgement is always important when we are mindful, just let things be as they are.

Be aware but not fixated on anything. Remember we are looking at things consciously, so we need to remain aware that we are just looking. If we become fixated we can slip into a dream like state which is not being alert and certainly not being mindful. When we are mindful we are aware of ourselves observing our world, you might say we are aware of our awareness. We become the observer.

Remember it is absolutely normal to find your mind wandering, distracted by thoughts, that's okay just gently bring yourself back to observing, seeing a colour, a shape or a movement. Noticing that your mind wanders and bringing yourself back into the moment is the goal.

Look at the scene, what can you see? Take it all in slowly but try not to give names to things so not thinking of the label we give to items such as 'dog' 'tree' or 'car' instead focus on descriptors such as the colours, shape, patterns, look at the finish is the item matt or shiny. This is can take a little effort when we first practice. The reason we do not find it easy at first is because nouns are integral to our language. We are taught to name everything we encounter, if something exists in our reality it must have a name, if it doesn't have a name it doesn't exist.

Notice movement, you might see people, animals or vehicles moving or you might see the movement of leaves on trees as a breeze passes by.

Pretend you are from another planet and have never seen such a scene before. How many shapes, are there? How many colours? How many patterns do you see?

Notice how you feel during this exercise emotionally and physically. Take notice of how you feel after the exercise both emotionally and physically.

SOUND

When my grandson was tiny, in fact for the first four years of his life, we lived a long way from him and his parents, but, we kept in touch via the internet with a regular video link. A friend of mine in a similar situation told me, that she used a brightly coloured rattle as an object of reference when talking to her grandchildren via the internet. From the time when her grandchildren who are twins were babies until they were toddlers, as soon as she had greeted the family she waved the brightly coloured rattle. As they grew and developed they associated the rattle with the grandmother, someone who they saw regularly on the screen, who loved them and spent time chatting with them and who several times each year visited them. I thought this was an excellent idea but instead of a rattle I chose to use my singing bowl. The bowl is made of brass and approximately 16 centimetres in diameter. At the start of each call I used to knock the bowl with the wooden striker/mallet and then run the striker around the top of the bowl to make it 'sing'. My grandson soon came to recognise the sound and when he was old enough to sit up unsupported to look at the screen he would smile as soon as I held the bowl up for him to see it. I would strike it and he would lean forward smiling waiting for me to make the singing sound. Whenever he came to visit he loved to get his little fist around the striker to hit the side of the bowl to make it chime.

Children love sounds, they especially like musical sounds that resonate with them. Tiny ones like to experiment with sounds. A wooden spoon bashing a cooking pan is great fun, and of course the sounds they can make with their own mouths are very entertaining. I recently heard a talk on skipping. As in skipping along the speaker was talking about the benefits of the activity of skipping which, we tend to think of as childish. I have to agree that skipping is a fun thing to do, and I also find beating a tune out with a wooden spoon and saucepan lifts the spirits immensely. My little guru and I have spent many happy afternoons bashing galvanised buckets as if playing the drums laughing our heads off at our attempts to making tunes up. We can learn such a lot of from the little ones if we are willing to search for our own inner child.

Whatever you are doing just pause and listen. Do not make judgements about the sounds, do not label the birds song as beautiful and the child screaming as bad or the clock ticking as annoying. Just listen. Sounds come and go let them ebb and flow around you, hopefully you won't have a pneumatic drill near you, because, whilst most other sounds come and go they do tend to go on for longer than we would wish for. Nevertheless even the sound of a drill can be the target of our mindful focus. Sounds we find disruptive or upsetting are only perceived as being unpleasant because we interpret them as such. If we shift our relationship from dislike to curiosity as if it were a new sound to us, and allow them to come in and out of our awareness the impact is lessened. This practice is especially useful if you are trying to work on something that you need to give full attention to and your concentration is interrupted by what you interpret as a disruptive noise. Just take a deep breath and observe the sound. It is all part of the world going about its business.

Mindful Exercise - sound

Make some time to just sit or lie down and listen to sounds. This can be done anywhere you feel comfortable such as at home, on a beach, in a town centre, the workplace, a cafe, or in woodland. Just listen without judging. Do not put labels on the sounds such as bird song, human voices, bees buzzing cars passing or horns honking. Just listen, be aware of the tones, the loudness, the rhythm in other words the texture of sounds. If your attention wanders, just gently bring your focus back to a sound and continue observing with your ears.

The next time you listen to a piece of music really close your eyes and listen to it. Note all of the different sounds that go into it, some louder than others, the different tones and pace, take note of how it makes you feel and where in your body do you feel it.

SMELL

Aromas can be very evocative of past times and places triggering strong images, memories and feelings. We know that some scents trigger happy receptors in our brains. I have been a vegetarian for many years but I still find the smell of bacon cooking very seductive and I know other vegetarians who say they also are tempted by that same aroma. This might be because it triggers memories from my childhood of full English breakfasts with my family.

It is well known that the aroma of onions cooking stimulates the saliva glands and gastric juices. Which is why people will stop by a hot-dog stall and make a purchase even if they are not really hungry at that moment.

It is believed that babies recognise the scent of their mothers within a few days of birth, a connection is made between the scent of the person's skin and loving care. I presume the same goes for the scent of their fathers or others who care for them. We know that babies like to nuzzle up to the neck area between chin and chest.

I can remember being rather worried that my little grandson was going to sniff flower petals right up into his nostrils and down into his little lungs as he stuffed his tiny nose as far into a rose as possible. He displayed similar behaviour with chocolate mousse which was probably even more worrying! We all have our favourite scents and aromas, on the other hand there are smells we do not like which again, varies from person to person. No matter what our preferences, I think most people will agree that smell is very important. However, in our busy day to day business, unless they are particularly strong we often do not notice the aromas around us.

Mindful exercises -smell
Take a few minutes to notice the aromas that surround you, no matter where you are there will be some smells around you. You might find it easier at first if you close your eyes and breath through your nose.

Choose a smell you like, such as a perfume, coffee a herb favourite herb or spice. Close your eyes and inhale (if using a strong spice take care do not hold it too close to your nose).

Notice what happens to your nose, observe the feelings the aroma stimulates, sink into the feeling and explore it. When the sensation fades choose another aroma and repeat the exercise, without judgement of good and bad but notice how the experience affects you.

TASTE

It is always delightful to watch a toddler experience their first taste of ice cream. They often look shocked at the coldness, pull a face of revulsion, smack their lips, then demand more. Our taste sensors are extremely complex not only do we have thousands of tastebuds on our tongue we also have taste cells in the back of our throat, on our soft palate, epiglottis and down the throat to the upper part of the esophagus.

We will come to mindful eating later but for now only consider taste. Try tasting something sweet, something salty, something sour and something bitter, note how each of the tastes affect you. For many years we were taught that different parts of the tongue had receptors for different types of taste, the tip of the tongue being sensitive to sweet foodstuffs, either side of the tongue at the front salty, behind the salty receptors sour and at the back of the tongue sensitive to bitter, tastes and the centre of the tongue being sensitive to savoury tastes sometimes known as umami flavours such as soy sauce, cheese, cooked meats etc. However, some researchers are now disputing what was once taught, that only certain parts of the tongue is sensitive to certain tastes. Putting aside the biology of how we notice different types of flavour, it is a fact that taste is important and preferences, likes and dislikes vary from person to person, as do our preferences for different aromas, smell and taste are very closely linked.

Mindful exercises - taste

Make yourself your favourite beverage, perhaps a cup of tea or coffee or maybe a glass of juice if you prefer. Take a sip and notice the temperature of the drink, notice the feel of the liquid passing over your lips, tongue and down the throat, see how sweet or bitter it tastes. Can you taste it in your mouth after it has passed into your stomach? How does the act of drinking it make you feel? Consider a hot day when you are really thirsty and grab a drink of water to quench your thirst. Compare the two experiences. One is enjoying the experience which is part of life, the other is functional and a few minutes of your life you will never have again.

We will revisit using our senses in later chapters. It is impossible to talk about mindfulness without incorporating the senses into the discussion. Our sight, hearing, touch, taste and sense of smell are how we experience the world we inhabit. Our senses keep us safe, give us pleasure, inform us of what we dislike and let us know where we are in relationship to the world around us.

Look, listen, smell, feel, taste, LOVE

3 EMOTIONS

I am not going to differentiate between feelings and emotions, because, I do not think it would be helpful to do so, neither do I see it as being necessary for the sake of the exercises in this book. Except to say that it is my belief that whilst emotions arise from events, feelings are learned behaviours that we tend to be unaware of until an external event occurs to trigger them. Emotions tend to be relatively short term whilst feelings are relatively longer lasting. The reason emotions tend to be short lived is because their purpose is to stimulate an action. I have heard some people would say that love is a feeling whilst joy is an emotion.

Children experience their emotions fully, be that happiness, sadness, fear, disgust, anger or surprise.

Watch a tiny tot's face when they are smiling at something or someone that makes them happy. Babies chuckles are infectious which is why even the most serious adult is often willing to make themselves look like a clown by pulling faces at a child or playing peek a boo with them. However, that delightful happy gurgle can rapidly turn into a furious howl. Have you seen the look of rage when something is taken off a toddler?

Even before they can verbalise, we know which emotion a small child is feeling just by watching their facial expression and body language. Later in life we learn to keep our emotions in check. We learn to not only hide what we believe to be negative emotions from other people, but we also try to fool ourselves that we are not sad or angry.

Burying emotions is not healthy because they always come back to bite us at a later date. There is very little point in being mindful of the world around us if we are not being mindful of our own inner state. Reminding yourself to take notice of your thoughts, feelings, body sensations and the world around you is a big step towards mindfulness. It is true that the more we work with mindfulness and gratitude the more peaceful we become. But ,until we reach the state of Nirvana (the final goal in Buddhism - a transcendent state in which there is neither suffering, desire, nor sense of self, and the individual is no longer subject to the effects of karma and the cycle of death and rebirth) we will experience the full gamut of emotions.

All emotions are based on dualism i.e. judgement of good and bad, love and fear, happy or sad.

One of the tenets we work towards with mindfulness is the understanding that nothing is truly good or bad. By which I mean, that it is the meaning we attach to things, places or actions that leads to judgements. To be honest, this is something that I still struggle with at times even though I understand the concept. The fact is we all have ups and downs in our lives. We all have moments when we find life difficult, times that are hard, stressful, painful and downright scary.

We do have days when we feel angry, hurt, anxious. Some people try to bury their emotions. They tell themselves that they are fine when they really are not. Other people try to distract themselves with other thoughts, work, concentrating on other people, or physical activities such as running, ironing or working out in the gym. Of course we can carry out these activities for pure pleasure or necessity.

Some people will use alcohol, food or drugs to avoid dealing with mental or emotional upset. Trying to avoid painful emotions doesn't work, it leads to greater suffering and steals our precious 'now' moments.

Instead of burying painful emotions we can go into the experience and clear it in such a way that we don't carry it around with us any more. It is only by going into the pain and treating ourselves with nurturing attention, that we can respond to what life throws at us, in a manner, that allows us to move on unharmed.

Mindful Exercise -shifting unwanted emotion

Once you get the knack of it the following is a really powerful exercise;

The next time you catch yourself with an emotion you would rather not experience, instead of suppressing it, trying to ignore it or distracting yourself (that never works in the long term). Take a deep breath and acknowledge the emotion whatever it is. It might be anger, fear, anxiety (which is a form of fear, as is guilt). Mentally say to yourself "I know that I am experiencing …. "(whatever the emotion) is. In common with everything else in life it is only an experience. And like all experiences it will come and it will go, just like the birdsong. Accept it, there is no need to go deeper into the feeling.

Be curious as if you were observing it in another person. By being mindful and accepting an emotion you can embrace it in your awareness, it is a way of accepting and loving your human self, and the experience of being human, which is at times, difficult. In acceptance and self-compassion we can find peace.

We can learn that there is no need to fight against ourselves, we do not need to feel bad about ourselves because we get angry or anxious or any other emotion. We are not our emotions, our emotions are part of the navigation apparatus that guides us through life. Physical pain tells us there is something amiss in our physical body which we need to address. Unhappy emotions tell us there is something wrong in our world.

Accept the emotion, with curiosity observe it, note where in your body you feel it, some people find it useful to silently name emotions, thoughts and feelings for instance "Here is that thought that my boss doesn't like me". Or "This is irritation" Or "This is anxiety" Love yourself for being human and let it fade away. Notice where in the body it is, rate it on a scale of 1 to 10, give it a shape, give it a colour, breath into it and release it.

It is not a good idea to tell yourself that you should not feel an emotion. It is easy to judge ourselves by thinking we should not become angry or disappointed by the actions of another person. Remember that an emotion is part of our feedback system. We are designed to feel emotions, the feeling of anger is telling you that something is not right for you. It might be right for someone else but not for you at that moment in time. Anger is a human emotion. What is detrimental to you is, being constantly angry. If you are angry all the time you are not listening to your feedback system that is telling you that you need to take action to help yourself. Hanging on to anger and resentment is very detrimental to our health.

When the emotion has left you, it might be helpful to investigate what was behind it. It may be an old emotion that has risen in response to a trigger, it may be something that you thought you had buried a long time ago that has resurfaced. It may be something in your environment that no longer serves you. Perhaps you merely had a natural response to an event that has occurred. It might be associated with your value and belief system that, does not match another person's. We are all entitled to our own values, beliefs and expectations. You might want to reflect on your responses to events. But remember to remain non-judgemental and loving of yourself. Remind yourself that you are not your emotions, they are just a part of how we feel our way through life. And, unless we hold onto them by constantly replaying events in our head, the emotion will pass.

Do be awarer that it is not necessary to examine every emotion that flows into our awareness. You will know when you do need to explore an emotion that arises and when you need to just let it go like a ripple in life stream.

To recap with a simple example, your colour, shape etc is likely to be very different. Let us pretend my family have left a pile of dirty dishes for me to deal with

Notice the emotion **I'm upset**

Give it a name **Its anger**

Notice where in the body you feel it? **Its in the middle of my chest**

Rate it on a scale of 1 - 10. **Its a 6**

Give it a colour **Its a murky red with black bits**

Give it a shape **A round spiky ball**

Look at it, breath into it for a couple of minutes

Notice the emotion leave your body. **Ahhh that feels better**

As I mentioned earlier small children have no problem with showing rage or upset. The action of taking a toy away from a small child just for a few moments in order to wipe away yogurt or pureed carrots from said toy, little fingers and face can, invoke a torrent of tears and screams enough to scare away a banshee. This is because small children live in the moment and in that moment they feel deprived of their toy. Once the toy is returned so do the smiles and gurgles. The child doesn't hold resentment for the rest of their life towards the person who took the toy away momentarily. But how does the adult react towards the child during the period of screaming? They try to shush the child, they tell them not to cry. We don't like to hear little ones crying, it distresses us. And this is how the child learns over time that it is not acceptable to show distress or anger. As they grow older they learn to internalise upset. I think the term 'suck it up' although not attractive actually describes exactly what we learn to do. And when we are sucking up the hurt or anger we are taking it into our energy field where it can be stored, added to and affect us negatively at a later date. Think of a sponge soaking up water, there comes a point where it can't absorb any more. So, it is important to register emotions, be mindful of how you feel, work through it and let it go.

Listen to your heart

4 DAILY ACTIVITIES

So now we have started to explore what mindfulness is about we see that it is the state of being aware of yourself, your environment and your experience within the environment where you are at any given moment. We have looked at the senses which we use to navigate through our environment and experiences. Our - touch, sight, sound, smell and taste and we have looked at emotions/feelings. Now we will start to put all these things together into total awareness which is also known as mindfulness.

At the end of an average day consider all of the activities you have carried out during the day. Then identify which of those activities you did in a mindless way. That doesn't mean you were careless, it means you were not mindful.

The following is part of a list I made of my own activities
Cleaning teeth
Dressing
Morning run
Showering
Dressing
Cooking and eating breakfast
Clearing breakfast dishes
Meditation

Making the bed
Turning computer on
Answering emails

We have now arrived at about 11 am and I have been extremely busy carrying out daily living activities. But, have I been fully immersed in the experience of living? Remember mindfulness is more than just a practice, it is a way of living. Mindful living brings awareness and caring into everything we do. And it helps us to cut down the stress in our lives.

Even a little mindfulness makes our lives better. What if, for whatever reason, I was no longer able to carry out these activities that I have listed? How much longing would I have? I am sure that if I could not carry out these tasks, I would find myself thinking back to times when I could do all these things. For instance, if I had no water to clean my teeth, I bet I would long to see and hear the water come out of the tap, I would remember what it looked, felt and sounded like. But, how often do we turn on the tap and clean our teeth on autopilot absolutely oblivious to the water running from the tap? If for some reason I was unable to run any more, I am sure I would yearn to feel my feet hitting the ground, feel the wind on my face, to have the awareness of the blood pumping through my body, to have the feeling of exhilaration on completing the run.

Sadly, we often do not take note of the precious things in life until for one reason or another we loose them. And when we do loose things, instead of being glad we had them for a while, we are often angry or sad at the loss. Have you ever had your electricity or water supply disrupted without warning because something has happened? Such as builders hitting an underground pipe they did not know was where they were digging? It happens.

I am aware that on the occasions when something goes wrong or when I have an accident such as dropping and breaking a favourite mug when washing up, or I scorch an item with an iron that is too hot for the fabric that I am pressing. It is always when I am not being mindful. I have my head in the clouds thinking about something other than the task in hand.

During the time of 'lockdown' due to the Coronavirus COVID19, due to the age and health issues of someone else in the household I decided that it would be prudent to keep away from public spaces and not take the route I usually chose for my morning 30 minute runs. Instead, I opened the gates either side of our house and ran a circuit using the back and front garden. As I ran, I was still able to be aware of the early morning chilly nip in the air. I eventually felt my body warming up to the point that I was able to remove my tracksuit top, I felt the breeze touch my skin as I peeled of the sleeves and I heard the thud as I tossed the top onto the garden table as I ran past, I heard the different sounds my feet made running on grass, and paving, I smelt the early morning newness with a hint of the salty sea. I was aware of the texture of my mobile phone in my hand, the earbuds in my ears and the music of the running app I listen to whilst out jogging. I saw the herring gull sitting on my neighbours roof his whiteness startling against a very blue sky. As I ran past the flowers in the garden I noticed the different shapes and colours and I suddenly became aware of myself as part of the landscape. If a drone had flown over capturing the scenery, within the picture there would have been a woman in a bright pink top running in a circle around a house, maybe looking like a tiny dot if viewed from high up. But, no matter how tiny we might be in the grand scheme of things we are part of the whole, we are part of the balance of this world and the great cosmos. Every one of us are part of he whole.

How many grains of sand does it take to form a beach? How many blades of grass to make a lawn? Every grain of sand, every blade of grass, every glittering drop of water in the sea around the small island where I live is important and they are part of the complete picture. To become mindful of ourselves as integral to the whole is very empowering. So yes, mindfulness is about focus on pinpoints of awareness but I think it is important to understand how that pinpoint of awareness is part of something much bigger. The scent of a flower fits into the context of the whole garden and everything in that garden including the sunny day, you and your emotional status. Many years ago a friend told me of a conversation they had with another person one clear starry night. One of them remarked how beautiful the night sky was and how when they looked up into the cosmos they felt tiny. The other replied that when they looked up into the stars they know they are part of it and it made them feel huge.

I am a strong believer of living in gratitude. Every morning, before I get out of bed I think of at least six things for which I have gratitude. Try it, I find it is a great way to start the day. It is impossible to get out of bed in a bad mood if you are feeling grateful for things in your life. Before you go through your gratitude list in the morning spare a couple of moments to be mindful of where you are. Lie still and be aware of your body, scan from the top of your head to the tips of your toes, your shoulders and arms, where your body touches the bed. Be aware of the linen against your skin, what sounds can you hear inside the building and outside the building, your own breath? Can you smell anything? Maybe laundry softener or the scent of summer air through a window. Bring your awareness to your field of vision, what do you see? Notice colours, light and shade, textures and shapes. Be present at the start and the end of your day. This is the 'now' that you are living, carrying out everyday activities is your 'now' be aware of it as much as you possibly can.

Love life

4 MIND WHAT YOU ARE EATING

We all know that we have to watch out for what small children put into their mouths. One of the ways they become familiar with this world is by exploring using their mouths. Everything goes into the mouth from the big toe to the rattle, blankets, shoes and other people's fingers are all there for the tasting. They love to suck, lick and bite whatever they can. And whilst they are getting their little gums around whatever comes into their orbit, they concentrate on the sensation of the texture and taste of the object.

How many meals have you eaten without actually tasting the food? I have to admit that I have eaten lots of food without tasting it. The reason being that I have been too busy thinking about what has happened or what I am going to do next to notice what I am eating. Food has passed my lips without notice. I find that going over conversations that have taken place and conversations that haven't yet but might take place in my head is a great way of being oblivious to life.

This is of course, a huge waste of time and totally mind less. If the conversation has happened it cannot be undone. We cannot take back words any more than we can unring a bell, and, if the conversation hasn't happened yet it might never do so. Therefor it is a waste of time imagining such conversations especially if they unpleasant and are likely to give me indigestion.

I have eaten far too many lunches whilst working, it was usually a sandwich with me taking bites between reading or writing information that could have waited for the ten minutes it would have taken to eat properly. I could have taken time away from my work to enjoy and appreciate what I was feeding my body.

Meanwhile, the food someone grew, someone transported, sold, cooked and served goes into our body hardly noticed. Sometimes we spend a lot of time planning food but what are we giving our attention to? We might be concerned about the calories, the nutritious value, energy content, speed of preparation or, if it is a takeaway meal the delivery time. But do we give any thought to where it came from and how it got from its source to us. And when the meal or snack is in front of us we often eat it without experiencing it because our mind is elsewhere.

Have you ever watched a toddler who has started to feed themselves, sitting in a high chair eating something like a banana? They somehow manage to get covered in it. Totally immersed in more than one way. They hold it in their little fists and squidge it through their fingers, feeling the texture, looking at how it changes from a soft solid to a mush. They might squeal with delight or giggle as they do so.

At this stage they have no concept of being separated from the rest of the world, they are at one with the squidgy mass. They smell food, taste it, they it feel with hands and tongue. Just watch a child who has something they enjoy eating, they smile and giggle, they feel in their heart-centre how good it is to have something nice.

I once watched my grandson as a toddler hit the tray of his high chair with a hand that was covered in food and then doing the same with the other hand that was relatively free of modged up food, I noticed that he was listening to the difference in sound the two hands made turning his little head towards the striking hand. He appeared to be fascinated by the contrast in the sound made.

Tiny children will drop food onto the floor, sometimes not because they don't want it but just to see what happens when it leaves the area of the plate or chair tray. It can be frustrating to pick up a rice cake that has been thrown to the floor and have the child howl at you when you take it away to put it in the bin. Even more frustrating when you replace it with another and just to have the same process repeated - floor, remove, howl. It is all part of the process and the child is totally immersed in the process.

You might like to experience mindful eating with a small child, join in with the squidgy mess, see what it feels like to smear porridge across a tray. Although, I suspect such behaviour might cause problems if we end up with a restaurant full of people playing with kids and food. As much as I love the image of that, perhaps the following would be a more helpful exercise:

Mindful exercise - eating

Choose a small piece of food you really enjoy which you can hold in your hand. A lot of people choose chocolate or a raisin, for the sake of this exercise I am going to choose a piece of chocolate biscuit.

If the item is wrapped in foil enjoy the feel of the foil, listen to the sound that unwrapping it makes. Hold the food item between your first finger and thumb. Bring your full attention to it as if you had never ever seen one before. Really look at it, truly see it, give it your full attention, observe every minute detail. Note the size, shape, colour, texture. Move it around so you see it from every possible angle. Notice how it feels in your fingers, what happens if you change the pressure of your hold on it? Bring your biscuit to just below your nose and breath in, notice any aroma it has. Notice any sensations the aroma brings to your body especially the mouth and stomach. Now bring the biscuit slowly up to your mouth, notice the movement of your hand and arm as you do so, the angle of the elbow.

Noticing if your mouth is watering as the mind and body anticipate eating. Open your mouth slowly noticing the lips parting and place a piece of biscuit into your mouth don't chew it yet, hold it in your mouth for at least 10 seconds feel it with your tongue, does 10 seconds seem a really long time? Now very slowly start to chew the biscuit be fully conscious about how it feels between your teeth, on your tongue, noticing the texture and taste. Put your full attention onto the swallowing process and how that feels. When you have eaten the morsel take notice how you feel after completing the exercise.

You might like to ask yourself how different this was to how you normally eat, and what you have learnt from the experience?

Of course if we applied this exercise to every mouthful of food we ate, we would take more than the time we often have allocated for our lunch breaks. But, we can build on this exercise so that we do become mindful during every mealtime.

By learning to eat slowly and deliberately and becoming aware of focusing on every aspect of the food, with practice we can truly experience our food no matter if it is a simple or complex meal or snack. We should always begin by looking at the food, being aware of the aromas noticing the texture and consistency before you eat. When the food enters your mouth noticing the flavours, the constancy as you chew and the temperature of the food.

If we are truly experiencing our food we are by definition not only avoiding distractive thoughts and distractions around us, we are also slowing down the pace at which we eat.

This slowing down and prevention of distractions has health benefits. It helps shift our awareness to the food, how much we have eaten and what messages our body is giving us, messages such as I am hungry, I have eaten enough, sometimes tis message might be this need for food is emotional not physical. Connecting with our bodies is very powerful. Our bodies will let us know when they require specific foods. Most people will be able to recall times when they have had an urge to eat a specific food type such as a salad or fruit.

We start to note how certain foods affect how we feel after eating them, some foods make us feel tired or sluggish some foods help us feel energised. It is not only our energy levels, but also our moods can be affected by certain foods.

We can also start to recognise behaviour patterns such as our relationship to certain food types when we are stressed or tired. Our relationship with snacks is also very important. Are we eating that sweet or packet of crisps (chips) because it is a habit or does our body require nourishment and if so are they the best choice for us? Just looking at the food before consuming it helps us make the right decision for us. And if we decide we do want to eat the chocolate or biscuit then eat it without self judgement but also mindfully and in gratitude for those involved in its production and transportation.

It should go without saying, but, look around any public dining area and notice the technology being used at the table. Please, no mobile telephone, no TV during meal times. It is impossible to eat a meal with mindfulness if you are engrossed in your favourite TV soap, quiz, talent show or news report. All the information on social media, the emails and the text messages will still be there after you have eaten.

I can remember when as a child growing up in the countryside hearing talk of city children not knowing where cows milk came from, and how horrified they were when it was explained to them the source of their daily pint. The reason this stuck in my memory is because I can recall one wit in the family commenting that it was a good job no one told them where hen's eggs came from.

Unfortunately many people have lost touch with where our food comes from. Unless we grow our own, it is often a matter of ordering what we want to be delivered to the doorstep or wandering around the shops deciding what appeals to us within our budget. I find my food takes on a new quality when I think about where some of the ingredients have come from and who has been involved in producing it.

Consider the humble supermarket purchased potato, just on a superficial level, how many people, how many hours of work goes into the bag of potatoes we pick up from the vegetable section of the supermarket? Someone produces the seed potato that is harvested, sorted, bagged and sold to the farmer who then has to plough and harrow the field, plant the seed potato, ensure it is regularly watered and checked for pests, the potatoes have to be harvested at the right maturity, they must then be weighed into sacks/bags some of them are washed prior to bagging, they are then transported to a distribution centre. Of course before any of this happens the farmer has to market his produce and come to an agreement and make a contract with the supermarket. Once in the supermarket somebody has to fill the potato shelf, and another person on the checkout has to take your payment. Let us not forget some vegetables are imported so a whole new layer of people involved in transportation come into play before we start peeling those spuds.

We can cook our food in a mindful way by being present in every action during the process, sensing with our hands the foodstuffs and the implements we use, noticing the aromas, looking at both packaging and foodstuffs, listening to all of the hissing, crackling, grinding, beating and bubbling sounds involved in food preparation. The more we practice the more we become adept at staying in a mindful not mind full state.

If you watch a TV Chef you see them fully involved in the process, they touch, smell and taste as they work. The respect for the ingredients they work with is what makes them so good at what they do.
In short, mindfulness food preparation and eating is being fully present, having no distractions whilst enjoying delicious, healthy food produced with love.

Nourish your body and your soul

5 OBSERVING THE NATURAL WORLD

The aim is to be mindful in all of our activities, however, making time to concentrate and try out mindfulness is a good starting point. The natural world gives us some great tools to practice with. How often do we go about our daily life without really observing and being conscious of our surroundings?

When he was a very small, my grandson loved to watch trees blowing in the wind. His mother discovered that on days when he was grumpy - as all babies seem to be occasionally, if he could see leaves on a tree moving in the breeze, he would stop crying immediately and focus on the movement in the branches. A few moments in a pram or high chair looking outside and the trees and wind worked their magic.

When my grandson started to walk, it could take half an hour to work our way 100 yards up the road. It can be tempting for the adult to hurry the child away from whatever they are focusing on, especially if you have planned on a specific destination such as the child's nursery, or a local park. But I never found this slow progress tedious because the delight of watching him stoop down, hands on chubby knees to observe a bumblebee on a flower was something not to be missed. The bumblebee or a ladybird on a blade of grass would hold his attention for a very long time. I could tell that he was taking in the movement of the insect, the contrasting colours, the buzzing of the bee, the scent of the flowers, maybe the feeling of a breeze or the warmth of sunshine on his face. He was at one with the world, seeing everything with fresh eyes. All those sights, sounds and smells were new to him.

On one hand we might view a child's world as being small. They have no concept of the 'wider world' all they know is what they see with their tiny eyes but once we grasp the concept of them seeing all the details of the world around them and when we understand that they experience the world as an extension of themselves and not something separated from them, we can start to understand what a huge world they live in. Once we comprehend that we are a part of this world, and the wider cosmos, then we can start to understand how enormous it is and by definition, how immense we are.

I remember a day when my husband and I took our then two year old grandson to visit the pigs raised at an old abbey. In the grounds of the abbey there was a sea of dandelions seeding. In the UK we call these seed heads dandelion clocks.

My husband decided he would show the little fella how to blow on the seeds and send them flying through the air. Today, just remembering watching the process makes me smile. The little one firstly needed to learn the difference between sucking and blowing, he then had to learn to hold the dandelion sufficiently far enough away from his mouth and not to stick his nose into it, it was a long process but worth the wait to see the expression of wonderment in those innocent little eyes as the winged seeds took flight and wafted away from him and sailed out of sight. Like most children, once he knew how to blow a dandelion clock he wanted to blow everyone he could find.

When I am digging dandelions out of my garden, I often think of that day. It reminds me to bring my attention back to the plants I am working on and to give them the same attention the little one gave to the dandelions.

Presently, I am lucky enough to live near to the sea and I can happily spend time sitting watching waves roll in and out, listening to the sound as pebbles are dragged up and down the beach, feeling the breeze on my face and smelling the salty air.

When I lived inland I was able to find activities that offered the same level of life enhancing mindfulness. Watching a bird in the garden or a buzzard flying and wheeling high in the sky, ripples of a stream over pebbles, just sitting and smelling the scent of flowers in a garden or park. These are the sort of experiences that shift our nervous system from jangling action to restorative serenity

Mindful exercises - natural world

1. Exploring the earth - go to a tree or flower, and imagine you have just landed on earth from Mars, you have never seen that plant or tree before. How would you familiarise yourself with it? Take in the shape, scent, sense it with your fingers, how does it make you feel? Note if you can hear any sounds around you? Really become absorbed in that plant or tree, explore it fully. It is also a living thing. Consider how it is nourished by the soil and the rain, how it has grown from the earth to maturity. Consider what other creatures live on or around it and what is their relationship to the plant. They might feed off it, nest in it, pollinate it. Ask yourself what is your relationship to trees and flowers.

2. Walking meditation - if you can do this barefoot you might find it enhances the experience for you. But if you have to wear shoes it is still a very good calming exercise which can be carried out either indoors or outside.

Because I believe it has many health benefits, I have added information regarding barefoot walking (earthing) following this exercise.

Start by walking a little slower than you normally do. Relax into the walking, feeling at ease. Bring your focus to your body be aware of lifting your foot, moving your leg and placing the foot back on the earth. Be mindful of the actions and how they feel. If you are barefoot feel the coolness of the grass, or the softness of your carpet or smoothness of flooring maybe the sinking into sand if you are able to do this on a beach.

Walk at a pace that is comfortable and allows you to maintain the mindful state. As your foot touches the ground be aware of the heel touching the ground then the ball of the foot and finally the toes.

It is very normal to have your attention drift away often. You might have thoughts pop into your mind or something in the environment might take your attention when this happens just bring the focus back to the walking without judging yourself, all you need to do is to acknowledge that you slipped out of the now moment, and then recognise you are back to being awake and start again with the next step. Noticing that our mind wanders and bringing ourselves back into the moment is the goal.

Walking barefoot in grass, which some people call earthing or grounding is a habit that slipped out of my consciousness for several years until one day it dawned on me why my small grandson was always so keen to run around my garden barefoot.

The reason is of course it feels wonderful. Did you know that some people believe that walking barefoot on grass can increase the feel-good hormones (endorphins) in your body and decrease stress levels by 62 percent? I presume it depends how high ones stress levels are to start with but I know that I feel completely stress-free when I am walking on grass without footwear. My favourite time of day to do this is, early morning when the grass is still cool to the touch. If there is a little dew in the mix I find it absolutely delicious to the touch of my feet. I must admit I do not walk barefoot outdoors on frosty mornings. Some people believe for full benefit that it is best to walk barefoot on the grass every morning and evening.

When we walk barefoot on the grass we are connecting to the natural energy of the earth. We know that the planet has magnetic fields and it is the energy from those fields of energy we are tapping directly into when walking barefoot outdoors. Apart from the feel great factor and our diminishing stress levels this practice is claimed to have many other benefits too including; helping to diminish chronic pain, fatigue, decreased muscle tension (which will of course help with some types of pain) and help to improve sleep

Our feet have reflexology points that relate to the organs of the body. When we go for reflexology treatment those points are stimulated in order to relieve ailments and to help our body to maintain health. When we walk barefoot we are gently stimulating those reflexology points. Our feet are connected to every part of our body even our eyes! The reflexology points for the eyes are the first, second and third toe.

Some studies suggest that walking barefoot outdoors can have other health benefits such as improved glucose control, an improved immune system and heart rate regulation.

The following is from the Journal of Environmental & Public Health published 12th January 2012

Abstract

'Environmental medicine generally addresses environmental factors with a negative impact on human health. However, emerging scientific research has revealed a surprisingly positive and overlooked environmental factor on health: direct physical contact with the vast supply of electrons on the surface of the Earth. Modern lifestyle separates humans from such contact. The research suggests that this disconnect may be a major contributor to physiological dysfunction and unwellness. Reconnection with the Earth's electrons has been found to promote intriguing physiological changes and subjective reports of well-being. Earthing (or grounding) refers to the discovery of benefits—including better sleep and reduced pain—from walking barefoot outside or sitting, working, or sleeping indoors connected to conductive systems that transfer the Earth's electrons from the ground into the body. This paper reviews the earthing research and the potential of earthing as a simple and easily accessed global modality of significant clinical importance.'

Walking in sand has health benefits, in addition to being a lovely sensation it can help our circulation which in turn can help nourish our nerves, muscles and bones of the foot and some people find it helps to reduce swelling in their lower extremities.

It should be noted that not all surfaces are recommended for walking barefoot such as hard surfaces like concrete.

If you have the opportunity and have not yet done so I recommend you try a little barefoot walking in the grass, it is non-invasive (unless you stand on a thistle or anything else sharp) it costs nothing and best of all I think it feels great. If you combine barefoot walking outdoors with mindfulness it can be pure bliss.
Happy walking

Another great activity when we can observe the natural world is whilst gardening - I have often seen garden ornaments and plaques with a written sentiment about one being closer to God in a garden than anywhere else on earth. No matter what one's spiritual beliefs I think we can understand the sentiment.

Gardening certainly gives those of us who enjoy the activity the opportunity to practice mindfulness. I loved watching my grandson in the garden at around three years of age. The concentration he exerted watering plants with his child sized watering can, always making sure that each plant received its quota of the precious fluid. When he helped me to harvest runner beans, he would take great pleasure spotting a bean of what he considered to be the perfect length for picking. In these sort of activities a child engrosses themselves in the task, they are not thinking about what happened yesterday or might happen tomorrow. They live in the moment. They live mindfully. By the time he was five years old my grandson had his own little plot in my garden where we scattered seeds to make a colourful wild flower garden. I have to admit the seeds did not necessarily get scattered very evenly but the joy on his face when he first saw his bright poppies flowering, he scrutinised their shiny petals and laughed when they danced in a slight breeze and took great delight whenever a he spotted a new flower appear in his bed. It didn't matter what variety it was yarrow or cornflower and if a flowering weed made an appearance it too was scrutinised and admired.

It is easy to look at a garden and take pleasure in the overall appearance of it but I believe that real pleasure comes from the details for instance really looking at the formation of a single plant, smelling the soil after rain, feeling the sun and the breeze and listening to the bird song, watching a bee going about it's business collecting nectar. In other words being mindful.

Pick a dandelion clock, cup it's gentleness in your hand and if you must….. blow the seeds into the world.

Love your planet its your home

6 JUST SITTING

One afternoon when my grandson was a tiny one, my daughter invited me to sit to the table and share a pot of tea and some cake with her. I glanced down at my little grandson in his baby bouncer seat. For those who don't know this is a sort of miniature lounger for children prior to their being able to support their own heads. They are made of a fabric support on a metal stand. Little ones are fastened into the lounger so that they lie at a slightly raised angle, these seats make a gentle springy motion with the child's body movement whilst keeping them safe.

My daughter must have noticed my reluctance to leave the child alone. "Oh, he is fine just sitting there looking around" she said. So, I reluctantly moved to the table a whole six feet away from him and looked back. Sure enough he was still happily having a little bounce and watching the beams of sunlight which were coming through the blinds and dancing on the wall.

How often do we just sit, and just be, watching sunbeams, just sitting and observing the world around us. Maybe on holiday or an away day we will sit outside a cafe and watch the world go by.

I am of a generation that was always told that the devil makes work for idle hands, so we grew up feeling guilty if we just sat and did nothing. A saying that is often heard in the spiritual community nowadays is 'we are human beings, not human doings', I think that this should be true, but, sadly, we are often too busy 'doing' to be a human 'being'.

We can sit with busy hands and still be mindful. Knitting, sewing, crochet, and wood turning are all activities that are conducive to mindfulness as are my favourite hobbies of spinning and weaving. I am sure you can think of similar sitting activities that allow for mindfulness. Activities where we can focus on what we are doing looking, feeling, listening observing ourselves within the activity.

Being in touch with how we feel whether that be at peace, joyful agitated, frustrated, satisfied. It is as important to observe what we tend to think of as negative emotions as those seen as positive. When an emotion such as frustration rises in you observe it, where you feel it, what it feels like, if it had a colour what colour would it be, if it had a shape what shape would it be, observe but not judge, you can love yourself for having that experience .

Sitting with hands occupied with an activity in which you can find mindfulness is excellent practice and can also be productive. However, sometimes it is good to just sit. Looking at whatever presents itself to you without judging anything (especially yourself) just sit, look, listen, take note how your body is, how is your posture? How are you breathing? How do you feel? Feel yourself part of the space that you are in. We pass through spaces all day long. Even during a day in our own homes we are in different spaces. We move from room to room but we do not consciously feel ourselves part of the space that we are occupying.

We might spend a lot of time and money purchasing a sofa or chair that is very comfortable but once it is installed into our home, how often do we sit on it and really sense the comfortable feeling of that item. Maybe for the first few weeks we do, but afterwards it is often the case we only notice how we feel on that chair or sofa when it starts to become uncomfortable, maybe the cushions become a bit saggy or the springs push through.

If you are a person who spends your life dashing around, organising other people and trying to fit 48 hours worth of activity into 24 hours, you might find sitting and just being, very difficult at first. Try just closing your eyes for a moment, take a deep breath to the count of four, hold for four, breath out to a count of four, hold for four and repeat. Do not try to fight the resistance because that is judgement of yourself. Just observe that you are feeling resistance. Notice how that feels, where do you feel it? If necessary stand up and walk around a little then come back to it. If you are not used to this type of practice remember that you are learning a new skill and like all new skills it might be something you find relatively easy or it might take a little practice to become adept at it, but it will come because it is a natural way to be. It is just that, we have forgotten how to be mindful.

I believe that very few people can be mindful all the time, the real art is in catching yourself when you are not mindful and bringing yourself back into a mindful state. To be able to catch yourself slipping out of mindfulness you have to be observant of yourself and that is of course mindfulness in itself

The next rainy day you have, spend just a few moments sitting watching the rain hitting a window, listen to the sound of the impact on the pane, watch the rivulets running down the window, be aware of yourself watching the rain drops, be aware of your body, your posture, your breathing and the rain. If your mind wanders, that's fine, just bring your awareness back to the rain, your body and your breathing.

Love just being

7 MINDFUL MEDITATION

As well as practising mindfulness in daily life in the myriad of ways already discussed in this book and those that you will think of yourselves, it can be helpful to set aside time for a more formal mindfulness practice such as mindful meditation. Meditation comes in many forms and there are lots of free offerings on-line that you might find helpful and there is of course a huge amount of books devoted to the subject of meditation.
My aim is to introduce you to simple tools you might like to try.

Preparing to meditate (If you are a seasoned meditator you might want to skip this first section)
Some people worry unnecessarily about the correct positioning for meditation. You really do not need to sit in the full Lotus Position to meditate. You might like to follow the procedure I am suggesting, but, basically the most important thing is to be comfortable and if you are able to, keep your back straight all the better. It is possible to meditate lying down, however, you might nod off to sleep which is not ideal so I suggest you find a comfortable sitting position.
This process can be used other than for meditation purposes. You might find it useful if you want to just take a couple of minutes out of your busy day to relax and collect yourself.

If you find thoughts keep popping into your head whilst you are meditating, don't worry, just notice them and let them go. When we try to force thoughts away they tend to become more persistent.

Meditation 1

1. Choose where you want to sit you might choose a chair, a bench or a cushion. Whatever you are sitting on make sure that you are comfortable and stable. I have seen people try to perch on a cushion chosen for meditation and wobble all over the place because the cushion was too high or not large enough or they have not sat in the middle of the cushion.

2. If you are using a cushion cross your legs comfortably, if you are sitting on a bench or chair ensure the soles of your feet are flat on the floor, legs and feet uncrossed.

3. Keep your spine straight but not rigid, let your head rest comfortably relax your neck.

4. Rest your hands on your thighs palms up or down depending what you find comfortable ensuring that you don't hunch forward.

5. Drop your chin slightly and let your gaze drop gently forward. Some people like to have an object to rest their eyes on. It is not necessary to close your eyes but some people do prefer to close their eyes. Beware though, some people find it easier for thoughts to float into their mind with the eyes closed. Maybe try eyes open and eyes closed.

6. If you are doing this as a short relaxation just sit and relax for a little while and when you are ready to just get up and go about your day.

7. If you are happy to continue this as a mindfulness practice scan your body from the top of your head to the tips of your toes notice any discomfort in your body, if necessary reposition your body until you are fully comfortable.

8. Bring your attention to your breath, breathing in and out through your nose, notice the cool air entering your nostrils and the warm breath leaving your body. Just watch the breath come in and watch it go out. It is natural for your attention to wander, that's fine, when it does just bring it back to your breathing. Don't judge yourself just be aware. Remember that noticing that our mind wanders and bringing ourselves back into the moment is the goal.

9. Don't try to fight off thoughts that come into your mind, just observe them and let them go. Anything we resist will persist, just keep coming back to the breath, following the breath in and follow the breath out. It doesn't matter how many times your mind wanders, just bring it back to the breath. The attention slips you bring it back, it slips again, you bring it back. And that is it. You do not need to do anything else.

Meditation 2

Follow steps 1 - 7 Bring your attention to your breath, breathing in and out through your nose, notice the cool air entering your body and the warm breath leaving your body. Just watch the breath come in and watch it go out.

It is natural for your attention to wander, that's fine, when it does just bring it back to your breathing.

Now count your breath in to a count of 4 taking approximately 4 seconds and breath out to a count of 4 taking approximately 4 seconds. Just, a nice slow breath in counting and a nice slow breath out counting.

Try to do four rounds of the in and out breath counting 4 seconds on the in and the out breath.
This is a beautiful stress buster exercises.

You might like to take this breathing a step further breathing in for four, hold for four, breath out for four, hold for four. Try to do four rounds

Love your mind

8 HOBBIES

Some people find meditation is not for them for a variety of reasons. If you are someone who cannot get on with meditation, don't worry there are lots of other activities we can engage in to improve your mindfulness.

I am going to suggest a few ideas and I am sure you can think of a lot more things. These topics could come under the heading of hobbies or pastimes. As the word hobby tends to mean something we do for pleasure or relaxation perhaps you can think of activities you personally find pleasurable and/or relaxing. Activities you already do or would like to try where you can incorporate mindfulness to give the activity an additional layer which will, both add to the enjoyment and also be beneficial for you.

Bird watching most people only see and hear birds at a subconscious level. We know they are there, but, we don't necessarily look at them.

If you have a window that looks outside, the chances are that you can see birds. If you have a garden or balcony you might consider installing a bird bath or a feeding station for our feathered friends.

It is not necessary to purchase binoculars and sit in a hide for hours at a stretch in order to watch birds. Of course some people do make a serious hobby of birdwatching there is no need to become a knowledgable ornithologist to benefit from watching and listening to birds. You don't even need to know the names of the various species of birds.

Just paying attention to the birds, watching their behaviours, looking at their flight patterns, listening to their songs and calls, noticing their colours. In other words just being observant builds our attention and brings tranquility to our lives. Try to be aware of yourself observing the birds. Remember that mindfulness is about being fully alert to yourself and your involvement in life.

Some years ago when I was employed as a training manager, I decided to have a bird feeding station erected to the rear of the building where I worked. It very soon became a mixed blessing. The staff group and students all enjoyed watching the birds and we all entered into the 'beat the squirrel' game. We discovered that we had a plethora of grey squirrels in the area, all of them wanting to dine on the bird food. The poor birds would not come to the feeding station when the squirrels were there. The bird feeder was moved to a variety of situations in the garden which we though would make it more difficult for the squirrels to jump from trees and hedge onto the feeder. Every type of hanging feeder was employed including a cage type 'anti-squirrel' feeder, petroleum gel was smeared up the pole to stop the squirrels climbing up from the ground.

We had an ongoing light-hearted war against Cyril the Squirrel and his family. We also had great fun watching the many species of bird that came to eat at our feeder (when it was squirrel free). A large poster appeared on the wall and the various species were ticked off as they were observed feeding.

I noticed that an awful lot of staff time was spent gazing out of the window looking at our feathered visitors. I did not begrudge the time at all because, it was my belief that a happy staff group is a productive staff group and it is important to look after the mental and physical health of staff and co-workers. Any mindful activity is good for our wellbeing.

Mindful colouring we tend to think about colouring in pictures as an activity for children. But, it is actually something that both adults and children can enjoy. In recent years there has been a growing market in colouring books for adults, it is sometimes called anti-stress art therapy. Let us be honest, most of us still enjoy colouring in.

I used to love colouring with my grandson, he would take great delight in opening a colouring book and looking for the pages he wanted to colour in. I was always ordered to colour one page whilst he did the opposite one. We used to spend hours sitting next to each other involved in this activity. There was always much discussion about colours to be used, and of course we a lot spent a lot of time admiring his work.

It is delightful to watch a child engrossed in keeping 'within the lines' often with a little tongue stuck out in concentration. Whether watching a child colour in a picture or colouring yourself, this can be a super mindful activity.

There are a wide variety of mindful colouring books on the market aimed at the adult population absolutely full of beautiful pictures waiting to be brought to life with coloured pencils. There are also some absolutely gorgeous pictures on-line that can be downloaded for free for those with access to a printer. The types of pictures identified as being particularly suitable for mindful colouring have a lot of fine details, they are often Mandela type patterns.

If you think that colouring in pictures is not for you what about painting seashells? It can be great fun to pick up shells on a beach (which in itself can be a mindful activity). Once they are thoroughly washed and dried the shells can be painted using whatever medium you choose ranging from felt tip pens to acrylic paints. Brightly coloured shells can be strung up to make the most delightful outdoor wind chimes.

The principle of mindful colouring is to bring your awareness to the present moment by focusing on how you choose and apply colour, you can feel your fingers holding the pen or pencil, listen to the sound it makes on the paper, watch the colour filling in the spaces, be aware of yourself present in the activity. As with all mindful activities the paying attention to the present moment brings a sense of well-being and relaxation.

Yoga - please do not think that yoga is only for the young with lithe flexible bodies. Yoga is for people of all ages and abilities it is an ancient form of mind and body exercise which can boost physical and mental wellbeing. The main components of yoga are a. postures (a series of movements designed to increase strength and flexibility) and b. breathing.

The practice is thought to have originated in India about 5,000 years ago and has been adapted in other countries in a variety of ways. Nowadays, there is a wealth of information available on the internet including videos that can be used to practice with for people who are unable to go to a yoga class. However, yoga classes are widely available in most areas ranging from beginners to experienced yogis. Some yoga teachers run specialist classes for people who need to remain seated.

Most yoga moves are undertaken in a slow mindful manner with attention on the limbs and the breathing. It is fair to say that mindfulness is an essential aspect of yoga practice and for me yoga brings a feeling of health, vitality and serenity.

I love that the 'child pose' is exactly what little ones do. I don't remember my daughter doing it but my grandson certainly did. Child's pose is a beginner's yoga pose often performed to rest between more difficult poses. The position stretches the thighs, hips and ankles and helps relax the body and mind.

There are many forms of yoga so, if you have not done it before, it may be worth while doing some research into what is on offer in your locality and speaking to the teacher before you embark on classes. Over the years I have found that I enjoyed some teachers classes more than others and finding the right teacher for you is important. Like most things, the more you practice it the easier it gets. So it is worth trying and don't give up on the first class.

Tai chi is a Chinese non offensive martial art, practiced for defence training, health benefits and meditation element. Some people refer to it as moving meditation. Tai chi is practised using slow, flowing movements which incorporate stretching and deep breathing. The person practising this form of exercise has to focus their attention fully on the movement of their body in sync with others in the class. Whilst moving one has to be aware of the in and out breath thus, making it a perfect exercise for enhancing mindfulness.

Running and walking are activities that really do offer an opportunity for us to be fully in the moment. I have mentioned running earlier. When first we had to go into self isolation in the Spring of 2020 I thought I would have to give up running which, was very disappointing. I first started running with the NHS (National Health Service) couch to five kilometres (C25K) programme. This is a free download audio programme which promised that over a nine week programme it would get me from sitting on the couch, to running 5 kilometres. The programme guides the participant from walking for one minute and running for one minute, right through to running non-stop for half an hour which, equates to approximately 5 kilometres or if you prefer 3.1 miles.

For the previous two and a half years I had done very little exercise other than walking. Previous to that time I had cycled, swum, walked and practiced both Pilates and Yoga regularly.

Even so, I thought that the C25K programme was ambitious for someone in their late sixties.

It was very hard at times but I completed the programme in well under nine weeks and found I actually loved and looked forward my thirty minutes run every alternative day.

Then along came a virus that meant we were supposed to take responsibility for ourselves and not get close to other people, and I thought my running was finished, I knew that if I stopped I would find it hard to find the impetus to start again at a later date. During a telephone call, a member of my family living in Germany told me about someone they saw on TV who had run the equivalent distance to a marathon on the balcony to their apartment. This conversation made me realise I could still run in my garden. However, when I first started to run in the garden I found that because I had completed my regular run numerous times I could physically run in my garden whilst mentally following my usual street and park route. The NHS app on my mobile telephone gave me regular updates on the amount of time I had been running for. Each time I received such an update I was delighted to discover that mentally I was about where I would expect to be on my usual route.

I congratulated myself on my physical and mental exercise. It took me about a week to realise that this mental exercise meant that I was not being present in my life! I was mentally running a recording of the past. And as has already been discussed, if we are mindful we are not in the past or the future but in the present moment.

Once I became aware of what I was doing I reminded myself to be present in the space where I was running, listening to my feet hitting the ground, feeling the air on my face, acknowledging what I could see such as the birds, clouds, plants etc.,

Sometimes I found myself thinking about what I was going to do with the rest of the day or other mind chatter creeps in, when this happened I just brought myself back to the here and now by listening to my feet hitting the ground and watching my breathing rhythm. I did not judge myself for allowing my mind to drift I just came back to the present and carried on. Remember the art is in observing ourselves and bringing ourselves back into the mindful state.

Walking offers mindfulness in many ways. I have already covered walking meditation which I highly recommend to those who find other types of meditation difficult.

If we walk in nature we can immerse ourselves in sights, sounds, smells, touch and sometimes taste. My tiny guru and I love to pick wild blackberries and if we are able to pick enough to bring some home, I do a little mindful cooking in the form of apple and blackberry crumble. I also make blackberry sauce to freeze and eat poured over pancakes or ice-cream during the winter months it is packed with flavour and a truly mindful experience when all it's rich deliciousness billows across the tastebuds.

When we have heavy rain, the lane near where we live has huge muddy puddles. My grandson and I out on our gumboots and enjoy walking through the puddles, listening to the swish of the water as our boots travel through it and the slurp noise when we pull our feet out of the very deep muddy bits. Great concentration (mindfulness) is required to ensure one doesn't fall over because the puddles can be very slippery underfoot and sometimes there are boulders to catch one's feet on.

Walking on sunny days is a delight. Looking at sunlight dappling through the tree canopy above, smelling the warmed earth, listening to the crickets in the grass or observing the buzzards circling in the sky and knowing how lucky we are to be able to be part of that amazing scenery is mindfulness that nourishes the soul.

Craft any type of craft work can be a mindful activity - knitting, sewing, crochet, jewellery making, weaving, pottery, painting, wood or metal work, or card making the list is endless. Any hobby or activity where you can focus on being present is suitable.

Creativity is an important aspect of the human psyche whatever form that creativity takes. Several pieces of research have shown that spending too much time using technology especially social media can have an adverse effect on our moods, whereas craft activities, carried out on a regular basis can improve our moods and feelings of relaxation.

Let's face it colourful stuff, especially if it involves a bit of glitter and glue can be great fun. In December of each year my grandson's first school invited parents and grandparents to help make Christmas decorations for individual classrooms.

Little fingers busied away with colourful paper, plastic scissors, glitter and glue producing what they thought were the most amazing and beautiful decorations ever to be seen.

Each cut out Christmas tree and paper lantern was held aloft with pride. Every representation of the festive season was made with love and the joy of creativity. Little eyes danced and little mouths chatted and smiled as they engrossed themselves producing their art. I am sure the adults enjoyed those afternoons as much as the little ones did.

Some craft activities have beautiful smells associated with them such as woodturning or scented candle or bath bomb making. Others feel very tactile for instance moulding objects from modelling clay, and some involve very colourful materials.

Knitting, crocheting, spinning and weaving all have a rhythm which produces a relaxing harmony between brain and body.

The important thing is to choose something you enjoy, you don't have to be an expert in whatever you involve yourself in. The point is to immerse yourself in the activity and let the daily mind chatter and worries go and just focus on the present moment and what you are doing.

Some people prefer to craft at home on their own and others like to part of a group. I can understand why there are so many knit and natter groups nowadays people enjoy the creativity and learning new skills whilst socialising.

If you are able to, make a creative space for yourself somewhere that inspiration can flow, some people are lucky enough to have a shed or studio and others manage just as well with a corner of a kitchen table with a bit of wall or pinboard to hang things on or for inspiring pictures or quotes. Whatever craft project you undertake become one hundred percent absorbed in it, only thinking about what you are doing, and only doing whatever it is that you are doing not multi-tasking, then you are being mindful.

Keeping a diary (journaling) People have recorded their thoughts, feelings and daily events ever since we have been able to draw and then write.

People keep all sorts of diaries, appointment diaries, learning journals, diet and exercise diaries, dream diaries, daily diaries in fact anything we want to keep a record of attached to a date and sometimes a time also.

Keeping a mindfulness diary or journaling as some people call it is somewhat different from other types of diary recording. This is because, it is a way to have an open and honest dialogue with ourselves. It is a tool to explore your inner self, to become more aware of your emotional self and the things that trigger you. It is a way of observing your life, your thoughts actions and reactions to outside influences.

It is a tool to facilitate you expressing yourself in a manner that is free from judgement, fear, or expectation.

It teaches you self-compassion, acceptance, and how to pay attention in your own life. Additionally, mindful journaling is useful for identifying moments and events large or small that prompt your mind into disengagement and into wandering away from the present now moment. It is all about training your awareness.

In addition to encouraging 'down time' for daily reflection, the practice of expressive writing has been linked with various other benefits including improved mental health, wellness, and productivity.

Mindful journaling is a great way to open an honest dialogue with yourself. It can help you become more aware of your emotional triggers, ruminating thought patterns, and even improve your meditation practice.

If you have ever tried to keep a diary to record events you will recognise that sometimes it is hard to decide where to start. Remember this is your diary, it belongs to you and you can write about whatever you want to write about.

Nobody else should read your diary or journal unless you invite them to, therefore, it should be a safe repository for your thoughts and recordings about your emotions. This reflective practice can sometimes bring things to light which we have been repressing for a long time. When things are brought out of the darkness into the light to be seen, they have a tendency to dissolve.

You might like to document your progress with mindfulness, noting how mindful you have been during the day, the things that helped you stay in the moment. Or you might like to take your diary entry time to practice mindfulness by writing about subjects such as the things that have made you happy that day and how that felt, or you might find it helpful to document the things in your life for which you have gratitude and why.

Maybe you can record how you have nourished yourself physically, emotionally or spiritually, and how that made you feel.

Your journal could be where you note the things you intend to do to improve your life and how you intend to set about doing them. Use your journal to write about anything that is to do with the internal you and how it links to the external world you live in.

Gardening has already been mentioned earlier but I think it is worth discussing a little bit more because **it** can be an absorbing activity no matter whether you are tending to many acres or just one small plant in a pot on your windowsill.

The observation of and meeting the needs of the plant involve an awareness of something in your environment, and your relationship with both the plant and the environment.

We can indulge all of our senses in our horticultural endeavours as well as our creativity. If you only have one pot plant on a small windowsill, you might consider decorating the pot it grows in. There are many ways of decorating a plant pot such as sticking seashells or beads onto it, decoupage or painting it. And of course you can turn such a project into a mindful activities.

One Sunday afternoon in April whilst weeding my garden I was listening to the BBC gardening programme on my radio, when to my delight two of the professional gardeners were talking about how relaxing gardening can be and what a perfect mindfulness activity it is.

I like to grow flowers but I also enjoy growing vegetables and herbs. Gardening activities can spillover into other mindfulness undertakings. For instance growing lavender can lead to making lavender bags. Flowers and herbs can go into homemade bath bombs. Seed heads from plants such as poppies and nigella can be gathered and dried and made into winter wreaths for doors and walls (this is great excuse to get the glitter out). If you have children in your life they will love joining with this activity.

Soft fruits can be harvested and conserved in alcohol. What could be nicer than a bottle of raspberry vodka as a Christmas gift? And, of course fruit, herbs and vegetables grown in our own gardens can become part of our mindful cooking.

Swimming some people love being in water and some people hate it. If you are one of those people who love being in it but rarely go swimming, perhaps it is something for you to consider. Most children take great delight in any opportunity to be in water, be that a swimming pool, a tiny paddling pool in the back garden or just splashing around in the bath even if they are not always so keen to have face, hair and ears washed.

Watching my tiny guru at aged eight concentrating on swimming two lengths of a swimming pool using the crawl method, focusing on his swimming style and using the correct breathing technique and then grinning from ear to ear on completion of the task was enough to remind me how much I can benefit from a regular pool session. Children do not need to be told that they are behaving in a mindful way, they just live mindfully from moment to moment.

I have friends who are cold water swimmers. They swim in the sea on the English coastline all year long. Nothing would entice me to even dip my toe in the water during the winter months! But those who indulge in this pastime tell me that it is the most invigorating activity and makes them feel totally alive. People have actually commentated that they never feel as alive as they do when they are in the freezing cold water. I am told that wetsuits are essential and safety precautions must be observed. I am not encouraging you to take up cold water swimming I am just offering it as an example of an activity that exemplifies mindfulness if we believe that being mindful means we are totally aware of ourselves and the sensations we are experiencing.

Fishing is not an activity that I know a lot about, however, my little guru and his daddy are keen fishermen. On a family holiday at a fisherman's paradise with lots of lakes stocked with various species of fish. I observed the concentration of those with rods and their obvious appreciation of the beautiful rural location. They were fully conscious of not only the water and what the fish were doing but also the other wildlife.

Music listening to other people making music or making one's own can be extremely important to people. Just sitting and tuning into the sound of music, singing or dancing to a rhythm, music however you relate to it, is a wonderful way to reduce stress, connect with your physical body and your breath.

There is music for just about every activity we engage in. Some people love the experience of singing with others in a group or choir. Studies show that choral singing improves our mood, leads to a decrease in stress levels, lessened anxiety and diminished depression.

We know that the deep breathing exercises used by people who practice meditation and yoga help to bring feelings of calmness, lowers anxiety and levels of depression so maybe it is partially the deeper breathing required for singing that contributes to the feeling of wellbeing as well as the feeling of comradeship enjoyed in group communal singing.

It has long been known that meditation, breathing exercises and music helps to lower blood pressure, increases blood oxygenation and builds stronger respiratory muscles.

I once had a client who belonged to a choir attached to a local hospital, all of the members had COPD - Chronic Obstructive Pulmonary Disease. The choir had been set up because research had shown that singing is beneficial for people with COPD.

Singing in a group gives us a feeling of being a part of something bigger than ourselves. The feeling of belting out a chorus of a song at a sporting or live music event gives us a sensation of well being, which is why people participate in singing with others.

A lot of people like to listen to gentle music when they meditate or if they are doing breathing exercises or practising an exercise such as yoga.

I often listen to music whilst cooking and I dance around the kitchen when there is nobody else around. My grandson and I have found that reggie is pretty good when we are cooking together.

Despite my advanced age I still love live music and I still really enjoy standing near the speakers at a live gig and feeling the vibrations of the bass hitting my body. I am not advocating this for others as it is probably not wise from a hearing or health point of view.

Preferred music genres are a matter of taste and depends on our individual preference and our moods. Most of the time we have music in the background, some people have the radio playing all day but only take notice when a piece of music plays that they either like or dislike a lot otherwise it is just background sounds .

Mindful exercise - music
If you have headphones put them on and choose just one piece of music to listen to. It might be a song or a piece of instrumental music.

Make yourself comfortable lying or sitting down. Close your eyes and just listen to the chosen music. You may be able to identify individual instruments being played, note the changes in cadence. Your mind will wander, just bring it back, don't judge yourself, just come back to the music. When the music finishes note how you feel. Do you feel any different to how you felt before you started to listen to the music.

Sit quietly, take a couple of deep breaths and hum to yourself. You don't even have to hum a specific song, just make a humming noise and let it vibrate throughout your body. How does it feel?

Love having fun

9 SLEEP

Cultivating a mindfulness practice, helps us, to establish a sense of general wellbeing which, of itself, helps us to relax at the end of the day. By doing mindfulness exercises before bedtime you can, lower your stress levels which, will help you sleep.

Anyone who has had trouble sleeping knows that trying to force yourself to go to sleep doesn't work. Have you ever worried that you won't be able to sleep?

Guess what happens when we become anxious about insomnia? Yes, we find ourselves awake most of the night! It just makes things worse and leads to frustration, anxiety and exhaustion and a further lack of sleep.

Sleep researchers tell us not to look at blue light screens for an hour prior to going to bed. Blue light is sent out to us from the sun, it is also emitted by digital flat screen TVs, computers, laptops, smart phones and tablets. Blue light is one of several colours in the visible light spectrum. The others are:

- Red
- Orange
- Yellow
- Green
- Blue
- Indigo
- Violet

- Together, they make the white light you see when the sun shines. Each colour in the visible light spectrum has a different wavelength and energy level. Blue light has shorter wavelengths and a higher energy level than the other colours.

Screen time, especially at night, is linked to poor sleep. The blue light from electronic devices disturbs our circadian rhythm (sleep cycle). It signals for your brain to wake up when it should be winding down. A simple way to explain this is, we tend to wake up in the morning if sunlight comes into our bedroom and we find it easier to sleep when there is a lack of natural light.

In one study, as little as 2 hours of exposure to blue light at night slowed, or stopped the release of melatonin. Melatonin is a natural hormone released into the blood by the pineal gland in the brain at night. Your body uses this hormone to help regulate your sleep - wake cycle.

Televisions, smartphones, tablets, gaming systems, fluorescent light bulbs, LED bulbs and computer monitors all emit blue light. So if you are looking at screens before going to bed it will take you longer to go to sleep.

If you have difficulty sleeping powering down your digital devices at least 3 hours before bedtime may help.

Some research in animal studies has shown that nighttime exposure to blue light may be linked to depressive symptoms.

But exposure to blue light during the day may have the opposite effect.

It has been used to treat seasonal affective disorder, or SAD. SAD is a form of depression related to the changing of the seasons. Some people believe that 20 minutes of blue light exposure in the morning helps ease SAD symptoms. Most of us feel happier on sunny days as long as we do not become exhausted by heat.

I believe it is especially important for children not to spend time looking at such screens prior to going to bed healthy sleep patterns are important for the child's development.

Mindful exercises - sleep

These exercises will help you move into a mindful state, they are not guaranteed to induce sleep, but, they will help you move into a state of mind more conducive to sleep.

One of my favourite exercises I often suggest client's try is 7:11 breathing. Quite simply you breath in to a count of seven and out to a count of eleven. Most people report they only need to do a few rounds of this and they fall asleep.

This technique works because, if you are counting, you are concentrating on the act of going through the numbers. This means that no mind chatter gets in to disturb you, at the same time because you are aware of the act of breathing and are managing it, the breath is being slowed down. By slowing down our breath, we are telling ourselves, that we are safe.

A message is sent to the brain to become calm and let go of any stress so we then relax our mind and body. It is impossible to breath slowly if you are being chased by a raging bull.

Get comfortable in bed if you are able lie on your back and take a couple of nice deep, slow breaths, breathing in through your nose and out through your mouth.

As you breath be aware of your lungs filling with air and your chest expanding.

You might find it useful to put your hands flat on your tummy so that you can feel it rising and falling with the breath.

Try to imagine you are breathing in beautiful sparkling white air.

As you breath out imagine you are breathing out and letting any tensions or anxiety of the day go.

After a few breaths of breathing in the white light and breathing out the anxiety or tensions check in on yourself. How are you feeling?

You might have all sorts of thoughts rushing up for your attention. That's fine, just observe them with curiosity and let them go, do not try to push these thoughts away, remember whatever you resist will persist, just let them surface and fade away. There is no need to explore these thoughts, just see that they are there and do not judge them.

Some people find it helpful to mentally pop their thoughts inside a balloon and let them fly away.

When you think the thoughts have subsided sufficiently that you don't need to give them any more attention, become aware of the points of contact your body has with the bed. The back of your head, shoulders, spine, elbows, buttocks, heels of the feet. Notice how you sink into the mattress. Mentally scan your body from the top of your head to the tips of your toes. Make any necessary adjustment to your posture so that you are really comfortable.

Notice any sounds inside the building or outside of the building. Just listen with curiosity, do not become hung up on any particular sound, just note it is there.

Bring your attention back to your breath, do not try to change the rhythm of your breathing, just be aware of your inhalation and your exhalation. Just observe your breath, note if are you breathing deeply, or shallowly, is your breath regular, or not?

There is no right or wrong, just observe it. If your mind wanders, just bring it back to the breath. Take as much or little time as you want for this part of the exercise.

Now you are going to run a mental video of your day starting at the point when you woke up. This will only take a few minutes. Can you remember how you felt when you woke up? Now run your video at speed looking at the elements of the day that come up.

You do not need to engage in or judge any of the days memories, you are just looking at them as if you were watching excerpts of a film in fast forward mode.

Remember these pictures are all history and you are now safe in your bed. If your mind wanders, just bring it gently back to the film.

When you have finished watching your snapshots of the day and have reached the present moment, run a mental body scan from the top of your head to the tips of your toes and make any adjustments you need to make yourself more comfortable.

And now run another mental scan from your toes up to the top of your head, take your time doing this, making sure each part of your body is totally relaxed and calm.

If you have reached the top your head without falling asleep just enjoy the sensation of being totally relaxed and comfortable and then let your mind wander freely wherever it chooses until you drift off to sleep.

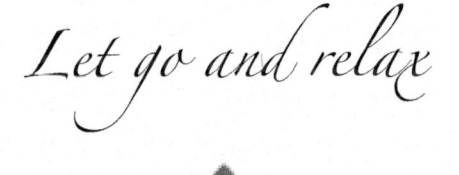

Let go and relax

❖

10 CRYSTALS

As someone who works with crystals for both healing and meditation, I would be very remiss if I did not to mention how helpful crystals can be to us when we are trying to cultivate our mindfulness practice.

In common with most children, my grandson has a fascination for stones and crystals. From a very young age he had his own bag of stones. And he loved playing with the collection of crystals I keep in my treatment room. He has also always valued stones picked up on the beach, in the woods or found in the garden.

I think that it is important for adults to understand that if a child picks a stone up and gives it to us, they are giving us something special. The world is still new to them and they are giving to us something which they recognise as being precious.

Remember, children are in a state of mindfulness, they see and feel all the nuances of a stone, if a bit of it shines in the sunlight they see that sparkle or sheen, if it feels smooth or crunchy to them they notice the texture, if it smells of the earth their little nostrils pick up the scent. They are aware of the colour and the energy and of all the stones on the ground they have selected that particular one.

So, if they hand us their treasure, remember that they are giving us a great gift. The same goes for the flower that gets picked by little fingers and given to us (usually with no stem). That stone or flower is a thing of beauty to the child who picks it and they love whoever they are giving it to, they love us enough to give us the treasure they have found.

Sometimes children offer their little treasures to complete strangers. Little ones love everyone and everything because that is all that they know.... love. How often have we heard or read that love is the answer to everything? As the human species, all we need to do is love each other and the world would be a far happier and healthier place.

Until they learn to be otherwise, children tend to be full of love and curiosity for everyone and everything. So many tiny gurus in this world trying to teach us this simple rule of the Universe, but we still have not learnt this lesson yet.

Perhaps the world would be a better place if we were all to carry a rose quartz with us at all times. Rose quartz is a stone of love. I find that it has a beautiful silky energy and has a lovely calming affect.

Many years ago a great friend of mine and I, were both employed as senior managers for the same organisation. Despite working long hours during the week, at weekends instead of relaxing at home, we ran a market stall selling crystals. I was a qualified holistic crystal therapist and my friend had also worked with crystals for some years.

We had a great fun and made a lot of friends amongst the other market traders. We enjoyed chatting to the folks who came to browse the market stalls. I wish I had a pound for every person who sidled up to me on our stall and confessed that they always carried a stone or crystal in their pocket.

Some People carry crystals for protection, some for healing, some because they get comfort from holding their stone and some don't know why, they just know that they like it.

We didn't make a profit from our stall but we did manage to break even and we had a lot of fun. Running the stall was such a contrasting activity to our day job, we both agreed that it was a therapeutic activity despite the early start and long drive to and back from the town where the market was held.

As well as enjoying my days on the market stall and the visits we made to crystal merchants, I learnt a lot about people and their crystals during that time.

The five crystals listed below are easily available for most people, they are some of the crystals that I would particularly advise people to use to help with mindfulness. However, it is necessary to remember that we all have our own energetic vibration and so do crystals. It is important to work with crystals whose vibration feel right to you. So please, use the crystals that you feel most comfortable with.

There is lot of information available on the internet, in books and courses offered regarding which crystals are suitable for specific purposes. I believe it is important to recognise that although this information is very valuable, it offers guidelines and should be used as such, rather than believed to be information written in stone (no apologies for the pun)

Most of this information on offer will be from people with lots of experience in working with crystals. However, even though I have worked with crystals for many years, I still dowse for the correct stone when working with clients rather than presuming that because a certain crystal or certain type of crystal has worked on one client that it is going to match the vibration of another person with the same condition.

If you are purchasing crystals, as a rule of thumb it is a good idea to go for the one that catches you're eye when you look at a selection. I find that crystals tend to select me rather than me choosing them!

Please remember the following are guidelines only, follow your instincts.

Amethyst tends to be a great all-purpose, master healer crystal. It has the ability to help us to dispel negative thinking and move into higher states of consciousness.

Because amethyst helps us to calm troublesome emotions and become balanced it is a great stone for aiding us with our mindfulness.

You might wonder how a crystal can help us with mindfulness. If we are unbalanced and our thoughts are scattered it is very difficult to get into a state of being mindful therefore, a crystal that helps us to gain balance can help us to be in the right state of mind to be mindful.

Rose Quartz tends to be a beautiful gentle stone. As I mentioned earlier, the world would be a better place if everyone was to carry a rose quartz at all times.

I find that rose quartz has a beautiful silky energy which is very soothing and has a lovely calming affect and helps dispel anger, impatience and irritability.

Known by many as the stone of love it brings us into the calm consciousness we need for mindful living. It is an excellent stone to give drivers who suffer from road rage. If we are angry we may not be in control of ourselves, if we are not in control of ourselves, we cannot possibly be in a state of mindfulness.

I am not saying we cannot be angry and mindful at the same time. We absolutely can. If I am feeling angry and I am aware of that feeling and am able to observe it, I am being mindful, I can be aware of my anger and my thoughts regarding the source of my anger, I can be aware of where in my body I am feeling that anger. Mindfulness is about awareness of ourselves in context of where we are in this moment of time.

Bloodstone tends to be a very good for helping with sleep and mindfulness, it works in a similar way to rose quartz insomuch as it is also a calming stone and helps to dispel anger, impatience and irritability.

Turquoise tends to help to stabilise mood swings and creates inner calm. Turquoise can help us to live in the present and not dwell on the past and to create the now moment we want.

Smokey Quartz tends to be an excellent crystal to have to hand if anxiety or stress pops up. Smokey quartz can be very grounding and can help us focus on the present moment.

In regard to mindfulness, we can work with crystals in a variety of ways. One way is to just hold and look at the crystal or stone. Take a couple of deep breaths and consciously look at it in your hand. Be present with it, look at the shape, colour, clarity or depth, some crystals have occlusions. Be aware of yourself holding and looking at the stone or crystal. When your mind wanders off just bring it back gently without judgement to the crystal.

Crystals are really useful tools for meditation, some people find that just holding a favourite crystal during meditation helps them get more easily into the relaxed state.

Some people find that having a pebble or crystal in their pocket helps as they go through their day. Just holding the stone can be grounding and bring comfort in stressful situations or at times when we want to remind ourselves to be mindful of the present moment.

Love gifts – all types

❖

11 MINDFUL COMMUNICATION

If we can communicate with people in a mindful way, our interactions become more meaningful, much deeper, and a warmth grows between us and other people which leads to life becoming a more pleasant experience.

When we speak about mindful communication, we mean applying the principles of mindfulness to the way we interact with others.

Communicating in a mindful way means we are being fully present and remaining open and non-judgemental during our communication with others.

It also means relating to other people in a compassionate manner. If through being fully present with them we are aware of the other person's feelings in the interaction, we cannot avoid being empathetic and compassionate.

It is only by being fully present with others that we truly connect, understand, and learn from the people around us.

When we communicate in a mindful way we are aware of all parties involved in the interaction including ourselves. Not just what we are saying but also the tone and the body language.

When we communicate in a mindful manner we are more aware of any emotional reaction our words create in the person we are communicating with and there is less likelihood of misunderstanding.

When we are speaking in a mindful way we speak as honestly as we can and are aware of what we are saying. We full engage our own emotional compass as we speak. We should be honest as is possible when we speak to others.

If we do not speak our truth we start to become judgemental of ourselves and the other person. The little white can come back and bite us. An example of this might be if you are out shopping for clothes with a friend or your partner. They might try on an article of clothing which you can see by their facial expression they love. But you might think it looks horrendous. They ask for your opinion and because you don't want to spoil their pleasure you tell them they look really nice.
Putting aside all the ramifications of what happens to the trust between you and the other person when, at a later date someone else is honest enough to tell them that the article of clothing doesn't suit them.
Your internal dialogue will be about your dishonesty and maybe encouraging someone you are fond of to wear something unflattering, not to mention their spending good money on what might turn out to be a disaster and something they never wear, so, you are judging yourself. Also, you may well be wondering how your partner or friend could possibly

have such bad taste, this type of thought means that you are judging them. If you have read this book up to this point you will know that our mindful practice avoids judgement.

Mindful Communication is about talking and listening for many of us the mindful talking is easier than the mindful listening. We can all tell when we are talking to someone and they are not actively listening to us. Oddly enough we can find ourselves in the position of having someone talk to us whilst our mind is flitting to what we want to tell them or our thoughts might be focused on other matters such as what we need to purchase for tea instead of listening to the other person.

The strange thing is we may tend to believe that other people don't know we are not wholly present and listening to them.

To become a mindful listener it is good to start with setting the intention to actively listen to the other person. This is important because if you set the intention you are entering a contract or in other words laying down a frame of reference with yourself so that if you notice yourself slipping into your own thoughts when someone is talking to you just bring yourself back to listening without judgement. It is human to let our thoughts wander.

As I have said several times already, noticing that our mind has wandered off and returning to the present moment is what we are aiming for. The art of communication is not just an exchange of words that hold thoughts and ideas but it also involves paying attention to what the other person is attempting to communicate beyond the words they speak.

We can gain the deeper understanding only through being totally present with the other person. When we engage in a deeper level of communication it opens up a true two way process and as I mentioned at the start of this section, interactions become more meaningful, much deeper, and a warmth grows between us and other people which leads to life becoming a more pleasant experience.

Let your light shine

❖

12 MINDFULNESS IN DIFFICULT TIMES

Mindfulness is one of the best tools we have for helping us through difficult times. If we can remain centred and mindful the external world has less impact on us. When we are focused on ourselves in the space and activity we find ourselves we are not looking at the outside world.

Many people agree that we live in uncertain times, it would be very easy to be pulled into a downward spiral of doom and gloom and believe mankind is going to hell in a handcart.

I am not saying that we should pretend that external events are not happening. However I am saying that we can manage ourselves even though we are not able to manage the world at large. If everyone was able to act in a mindful manner there would be no global problems let alone local ones. So if we all work on ourselves we can start to have a positive impact on our own little piece of this world.

Sometimes when I am working with clients who come for therapy sessions, they comment about how difficult they find it to remain mindful when their thoughts are constantly drawn into the difficulties they are currently dealing with.

I understand this difficulty however when we start to look at said difficulties they are usually around issues of the past or fears of what might happen in the future be that eminent or in the long term.

Some people find that they are constantly remembering and thinking about traumatic things that have happened to them in the past. In addition to using therapeutic interventions which I have been trained to use, I always encourage people to try to be in the moment.

I encourage them if they are battling with old memories, to tell themselves that whatever happened did happen, but it happened in the past not in this now moment.

We need to tell ourselves that in this now moment nothing bad is happening to us. In this now moment we are perfectly safe, nothing awful is happening in this now moment, nothing is hurting us in this now moment. In this now moment there is nothing to be scared of because, everything is perfect in this now moment. Feel this now perfect moment and recognise that we have one perfect moment after another.

Exactly the same principle applies when we become anxious about things that might happen.

Yes, something horrible might happen in the future. However, it is not happening in this moment, it may never happen, it is not happening in this moment, this moment is perfect we are safe.

Projecting ourselves back to old events can be very painful. Sometimes we look back at happy times and feel sad because we have lost something or someone from that happy time.

Sometimes we look back at unpleasant events that have happened to us such as someone hurting us in some way or other. Of course we should acknowledge those things in our lives that have led us to the present moment in time. Our history is part of what makes us the people we are.

As a therapist I am very aware that it is not healthy to bury feelings and fears, and when there is a root cause in the past that has led to a present problem, we absolutely need to address it.

However, if something occurred in the past that hurt us emotionally, if we re-live that event it will hurt again. And if we keep re-living it, it will keep hurting again and again each time we re-live it. The question is, how many times will you put your hand into the same fire before you stop wanting to be burnt by it?

We can all find ourselves looking back fondly to people who were once in our life but are no more, or we might look back at places we have visited or lived in, cars we have driven, people we have known, experiences we have had, and all sorts of other happy memories. It is nice to revisit happy memories now and again. It is for that reason we keep photographs either physical prints or digital images.

However, beware, there is a difference between remembering the past with pleasure and wallowing in nostalgic thoughts. Scientists say that each time we remember something the memory changes slightly We don't do this on purpose but instead it's an involuntary side effect of the process of activating memories. Maybe you are reading this and because you have an excellent memory, you are thinking that this does not apply to you. Caste your mind back, have you ever had a discussion with someone regarding a shared memory and been surprised to discover that the other person has a different version of what happened? It happens all the time in families. People disagree about where an event happened, what the occasion was or who said what.

So if we think about it, we can see that it is possible that, the memory of the event that keeps haunting a person may not be an absolute true representation of what happened. In which case they are allowing a false memory to ruin their now moment. But, as I mentioned earlier if an issue is caused by a past event, it is important for us to ensure that root cause is healed.

One of my favourite quotes is from Lao Tzu:

*"If you are depressed you are living in the past
If you are anxious you are living in the future
If you are at peace you are living in the present"*

This quote very neatly encapsulates just about the main message of this book. Lao Tzu (Laozi) was an ancient Chinese philosopher and writer, he is believed to have been the founder of philosophical Taoism, and a deity in religious Taoism and traditional Chinese religions. He is the reputed author of the Tao Te Ching which is also known as The Book of The Way or The Book of Integrity depending on the translation. It is thought that the Tao Te Ching was written approximately 400BCE it contains 81 verses of wisdom regarding how one can live with goodness and integrity. If he was the author of the Tao Te Ching (we have no reason to doubt this) Lao Tzu was not his actual name because translated it means Old Master and by definition this is not a name one has throughout life. It is probable that his name has become lost in the mist of time. I believe that this Taoist quote helps to confirm my earlier point that what we now call mindfulness is an integral part of many belief systems. But, let us not underestimate it's important role in the secular if we want to live a full enriched life.

Mindfulness is empowering because it is something we do for ourselves. It is not an external intervention imposed on us. Even if we attend a course or workshop to learn techniques to improve our practice those teaching us are not doing anything to us, they are facilitating our understanding of how to better help ourselves. We have a choice to use the techniques or not.

When we find ourselves experiencing difficult times, it is extremely important that we maintain a grounded, empowered and centred state of mind. The more skilful we are in living in the moment, and having a clear view of everything that is happening within our experience, the easier we are able to remain calm and cope with difficult situations without becoming stressed and allowing our emotions to spin out of control.

The more we practice mindfulness, the easier it becomes to live in the present moment so that we are fully aware of ourselves, our environment and our presence within our environment. We can then avoid living in the past and becoming depressed. We can also avoid becoming anxious due to projecting our thoughts into a future where fear exists.

It is a fact that what we resist will persist, it is also true that whatever we put our attention on is what finds its way to us. The trouble is, we forget to observe our thoughts and emotions. It is a fact that it is impossible to push thoughts away in the long term.

We can fool ourselves that we are keeping unwanted thoughts out of our mind by finding things to occupy our mind. We hear people say "Oh I just keep myself busy so that I don't think about …." Unfortunately those issues and the associated thoughts are still running in the background, waiting to jump out at us. And they do jump out at us, they keep resurfacing, often in the middle of the night. It might sound trite, but the old saying that is often quoted 'what you resist will persist' is very true.

If we become aware of those sneaky thoughts and examine them we can deal with them. Let us look at a hypothetical scenario. A person believes that their work is being scrutinised by their employer or work supervisor. They could decide that they are being observed because they do such a great job and maybe they could be in line for a promotion. But in this instance they don't think that, no, they decide that the boss wants to get rid of them and that supervisor is waiting for them to make mistakes. Their imagination then goes into overdrive and the memory becomes razor sharp. They remember every conversation they have ever had with their boss which could be misconstrued to be a criticism of their work. They then start to think of differences of opinions they have had with co-workers. They start to see a conspiracy against them. And thus the person goes into a downward spiral until they start to make errors at work, and, we can guess where the story will go from there.

And so we need to get out of our heads and into the business of living in the moment.

It is easy to get caught up in other people's perception of world events. Social media, the mainstream media and the alternative media are all vying for our attention and it is very easy to get sucked into the fear cloud. I find it helpful to avoid such attention clamouring and when I do get pulled in I ask myself the following questions;

Can I do anything with this information?
Is this helpful to me?
Is this helpful to anyone else?
Is this harmful to me?
Is this harmful to anyone else?

Allow yourself to feel good all the time

❖

13 LOST DOWN THE TECHNICAL RABBIT HOLE

I believe that one of the biggest hindrances to mindfulness nowadays is the mobile device. Some of us have our heads permanently half cocked listening for 'the ping.' That sound that lets us know that we have a reply to a text, or an incoming email that requires an immediate response. Or that someone has put some riveting information on a social media site. It could be a video of a cute cat answering the doorbell or maybe a photo of someone's lunch. Let us be honest, that electronic ping sound from email or social media is very hard to ignore. But, do we want our life to be run by our electronic devices?

I would like to suggest that it a good idea to have a set time for social media and email. If someone is desperate to talk to you at 7 O'Clock in the evening they will call you. In every moment we have choices, we can choose to answer the telephone or not. No-one has the right to your time and attention, neither should we be upset if people don't give us an immediate response to our electronically sent messages.

Have you heard of Pavolov's dog experiments?

You may have, but let me remind you, and explain why I think his experiments are pertinent to some of our stress factors today and further how this relates to mindfulness or lack of mindfulness. Cutting a long story short Ivan Pavlov was a Russian physiologist who won the Nobel Prize in 1904 for his work studying digestive processes.

His work on digestion lead to one of the most important discoveries in psychology and still helps us to understand human behaviour today. And, like a lot of important discoveries it was discovered by chance.

The concept of what is today known as classical conditioning. Classical conditioning is studied by psychology students still today. Interestingly Pavlov was a physiologist not a psychologist.

Pavlov noticed that the dogs he was working on salivated every time an assistant came into the room. The assistants gave edible and non-edible items to the dogs whenever they entered the area the dogs were kept in.

Pavlov realised that even when given non-edible items the dogs still salivated because they associated the assistants with food/tidbits. He came to the conclusion that the salivation was an automatic response not caused by the sight or smell of food but, by the sight of the source of food i.e. the assistants.

He did various experiments he used a metronome and sure enough the dogs responded to that sound and associated it with food. We tend to hear about Pavlov's dogs salivating to the sound of a bell. This is because he used a bell as a neutral sound for the dogs to respond to and associate with food. This he did through having a bell rung prior to the dogs being given food. The dogs came to associate the sound of the bell and food. The salivating was an automatic response to the sound.

So what does this have to do with us today and our stress levels and mindfulness? Well, we also fall prey to classical conditioning. Sometimes it is what keeps us safe. It is about learning from the environment.

You eat something that makes you ill, do you want to try it again the next day? Of course not! Even though it may have been that on the one occasion there was a problem with the food not your ability to tolerate it. If you touch something hot and burn your hand on it, you tend to be more careful next time. If someone walked towards you carrying a hot item you would step away or to the side, this is an automatic response. We become conditioned.

Have you ever been out in a public area and noticed how people respond to a notification chime on a mobile phone? You will see people automatically reach for their phone even if it is not theirs that has pinged or chimed a notification.

The notification sound is a neutral stimulus the same as the metronome or bell. People have become conditioned to associate the notification sound with the positive feeling of reading a message. When we have this sort of an automatic response to a sound we are not acting in a mindful way but with an automatic response.

Technology can greatly enhance our lives but there can of course be a downside to this. It might be that we hear the chime or ping of an email and our heart sinks because we believe it is work being piled onto us.

There can be fear of being in trouble if we do not respond immediately. Nowadays people often expect immediate answers to emails and messages. Some people become stressed if that response is not given immediately, and of course the stress levels go up in the person not receiving the response. If the receiver of the message or email are unable to provide an immediate reply for whatever reason their stress levels can be raised just by knowing someone else expects an immediate response.

Consider electronic hygiene. How much of your time and energy do you want to give to an electronic device? Can you turn it off and look at the real world?

When we are busy going down rabbit holes searching for information we can become totally focused on the job in-hand but not necessarily mindful. The internet can be a wonderful source of information but one article or site can lead you to another and that leads to another and so on, and thus we get lost in the time and attention stealing rabbit hole.

The same principles apply to the playing of electronic games to which a lot of both adults and youngsters appear to be addicted. We can loose track of time, ignore our bodies requests for sleep, fresh air, exercise and even food. This really is a lack of mindfulness.

I have already mentioned people in cafes and restaurants ignoring their children as they focus on their mobile devices but, we all know it doesn't stop there. People walk through shopping malls or on streets with their eyes and fingers busy with the cyber world appearing to be totally oblivious to life going on around them.
I have even seen people in places of beauty such as the sea shore and in gardens open to the public doing exactly the same thing, eyes fixated on a hand held device not even having a 'voice to voice' conversation with another human being.

One of the major problems I see in the rabbit hole of the cyber world is the temptation to fall into benchmarking. I think it is really difficult not to 'benchmark' or in other words compare our lives with those of others.

The making of comparisons has always occurred but the cyber world encourages us to do it even more. This judging our lives and ourselves against others all starts when we are small children. Offspring are often compared to children of our friends or family members. Comparisons are made about the age at which they start to take solids in their diet, crawl and walk or when they start to speak.

If we don't compare our babies development with that of other the medical profession will be happy to do it for us. I appreciate that some parents do find it reassuring to know that their child's development is on track so to speak, but, how many parents become distressed because someone has told them "At this age your child should be able to do XY and Z" and the child has not yet 'performed' to that standard?

Even primary schools in the area I live have 'star pupils' named each week during assembly.
And if your child practices their times table using an on-line device, they can be the TT Rockstar of the week.

We then have art and writing competitions, Easter bonnet competitions, house points and on it goes until, we find ourselves as adults comparing ourselves to others. We compare our jobs, cars, housing etc. Some of us may be counting how many followers we have on social media and comparing ourselves to other social media users.

When we are young we are compared to our siblings, friends and the kid down the street, who is the tallest, cleverest, fastest, muckiest or the most polite etc. So it is not surprising that we learn to compare ourselves and our lives to that of others. And let us face it, nowadays it seems as if everyone wants to share every detail of their lives with us via social media.

When we are focusing on other people and their lives we are not fully engaged in the business of living our own life. Our attention is being pulled elsewhere and we can easily fall into the trap of believing our lives are less enriched than those of others.

I think we should recognise that when people are posting on social media sites, they have either got into the habit of sharing every minute of their life with the world (this may be for all sorts of reasons) or they just want to share a snapshot or highlight of their life.

Although other people's motivations for posting on their page is not our business knowing we are only seeing a snapshot of their life put things into perspective. What really matters is the how it affects us and how we interpret those words and pictures, how we use that media to make judgements/comparisons with our lives.

We are all human beings, we all have our strengths and we all have things which we are not so good at as others.

We all have joys, troubles and tribulations, we all have laundry to do, meals to cook and toilets to clean. I am not saying that we should be cynical about other people's joys and happy postings on social media but, I am saying do not compare their life to yours, it is just a glimpse of their life.

If someone is sharing a happy moment on social media be happy for them, share their joy.

If we accept that other people want to share their happiness and delight in life with us and if we can embody that feeling they are sharing, it can only enrich our lives.

When we say to someone 'I am so happy for you' if it comes from our heart we feel good too. If you cannot do that and if you find that social media makes you feel unhappy, jealous or discontented then simply unplug from it.

So, what does this all boil down to? We can appreciate other people, their gifts and good fortune without comparing ourselves to them.

When we hear of a person we went to school becoming very successful in an area of their life, we can be happy for them without diminishing ourselves. It is just part of their life.

Because for a moment in time someone else appears to 'have it all' we should never, ever, feel diminished or that our life is 'less than enough.' We all 'have it all' sometimes.

Undoing the habit of comparing ourselves to others which starts in early childhood is not easy, but when we do, we become freer, happier, more balanced and content in our life.

The happier we are the more we get out of life and the more we can achieve.

When we don't compare ourselves with others we stop worrying what others will think and that gives us a lot of freedom to do what we want, how we want, when we want.

If we find ourselves looking outwards at other people's lives and making negative comparisons it is maybe a good idea to be aware that we are doing so. And then look at those things in our life that make us happy, people, places objects.

Of course we have to live in the real world and it is a fact that there are times when we are less contented or less happy than others. However, I believe it is a helpful practice when we find ourselves feeling despondent because of real or imaginary comparisons for us to just be aware of being affected by these external factors. Because when we are aware, we are mindful.

When we negatively compare ourselves to others, we are bringing external factors - real or imaginary into ourselves, internalising stuff that we don't need to.

I say real or imaginary because when we are comparing ourselves or our lives to others we don't really know all the facts about the other person.

So if we notice those feelings, look at them without judgement, never try to push things down or away because if you do that, they keep popping back up.

Remember that the technique of observing emotions is an excellent mindfulness technique.

We look at the emotion and acknowledge without judgement it is there, "Oh I am feeling jealousy," what does it feel like?

How sever is it on a scale of 1 - 10? (1 being nothing much 10 being as bad as it gets)

Where in the body has it settled?

If it had a colour what colour would it be?

If it had a shape what shape would it be?

Can you let it wash through you down into the ground? It is surprising how when we look at an emotion it disappears. And let's face it non of us want to carry around a load of unhappy emotions. The next step is to think of something or someone you really love or feel joy about. It might be your happy place or a happy memory of the past. Think about it, some people find it helps to place a hand on their body in the heart centre.

Let that happy thought really sink into you.

Where do you feel it, if it had a colour what colour would it be?

If it had a shape what shape would it be?

Can you allow that happy feeling to completely fill you up? Do you see how it takes just a few moments to look at an emotion and let it go or let it fill you up?

I think it is a good idea if we let go of an undesirable emotion or feeling, to replace it with a happy one. The more we observe our emotions the easier it becomes.

Although I am inviting you to explore the dangers of the cyber world, please do not think that I am some sort of old fashioned Luddite.

I am extremely fond of technology.

I love that I can talk to my friends and family around the world, not only talk but we can see each other and chat in real time, anywhere in the world.

I love that I can share photographs and other information at the click of a button.

I love that I can hear just about any type of music no matter where I am, and I can watch films/videos at a time to suit me not just when it is being programmed for showing.

In August 2021 I spent a week on holiday in a location with no internet and very little telephone reception.

There was a television available with terrestrial programmes however, I rarely watch TV and that week was no exception.

It was very odd at first to not have that instant connection with the outside world but, it was very liberating and meant that I was truly immersed in the experience of being with my family in a very beautiful location.

If you are someone who finds it hard to detach from the cyber world you might try a cyber detox for two days. The first day to adjust to the lack of internet and the second day to really enjoy the feeling of liberation.

You might feel tempted to extend your detox.

If you really cannot function without the internet, maybe try just taking a break from social media.

Let yourself be free

14 THANK YOU WORLD, UNIVERSE, ANGELS, GOD - or whatever you believe in

It is impossible to have gratitude without at the same time being in a state of mindfulness When we are consciously appreciating something in our life, in that moment of time, we are focused on whatever it is that we are appreciative of. In other words, gratitude and mindfulness go hand in hand. However, it is worth spending a little time exploring what we mean when we use the term 'gratitude'. It is a fact that when we live in a state of gratitude, we become more content and thus happier. If you listen to modern Gurus such as Wayne Dyer, Bruce Lipton and Greg Bradon, or Eckhart Tolle you will hear them talking about the importance of gratitude. There is nothing new about the concept that gratitude improves our levels of happiness. The ancient wise ones knew about and understood the importance of gratitude, I have a list of wonderful quotes but here are just a couple of them;

"A grateful mind is a great mind which eventually attracts to itself great things." - Plato

"He is a wise man who does not grieve for the things which he has not, but rejoices for those which he has." - Epictetus

The following is attributed to Buddha and always makes me smile

"Let us rise up and be thankful, for if we didn't learn a lot today, at least we learned a little, and if we didn't learn a little, at least we didn't get sick, and if we got sick, at least we didn't die; so, let us all be thankful."

Gratitude can be a spontaneous feeling but, studies have shown that it can be deliberately cultivated and that there are both social and individual benefits to cultivating gratitude. What do we mean when we say cultivating gratitude? Put simply, it is looking for things to be grateful for. There is an old saying about not appreciating things and people until they are gone. Surely it is a better idea to be aware of the good things in our life whilst they are there rather than waiting until they are gone.

When we cultivate gratitude, we look for things to have gratitude for all the time. We don't overlook all the small things that make our life go smoother. Those little things that make our life richer than it would be without them. Things like a friend calling just to say hello, a bird singing outside the window, a bus coming along just as we get to the bus stop, a colleague offering to make a cup of tea or coffee when yo are too busy to make your own, seeing the first buds of Spring.

Anyone who has dropped a mobile phone, had one get wet or just stop working knows how frustrating it is not to have that device whilst waiting for it to be either repaired or replaced. But how often do we think how lucky we are to have such instant communication with others and to have such a lot of information at our finger tips, people's contact information easy to find so we don't need to thumb through an address book, the fact that we can take and keep photos, look information up in a split second. Our mobile devices do such a lot but some of us take our mobile phone for granted. Likewise our health, our family, our senses, the food we eat and the clothes we wear. But take any of these things away and how would we feel?

It is easy to flick a switch and turn on the light or oven, most of us are so used to the utility services and it is only when we have a disruption to the service such as a burst pipe or power cut that we appreciate what we normally take for granted.

Gratitude is an emotion and it is one that makes people feel happier, so it is a feeling, a mood of well being It's an emotion that builds an aura of positivity around us which not only makes us feel good but it also radiates out to other people who also feel more positive and happy in our company.

Studies show that practicing gratitude stops us using the sort of words that express negative emotions, and when we don't use negative words we shift our inner attention away from negative emotions such as resentment, anger and envy.

We know that if we use phrases such as I'm fed up, I hate my job, I'm bored, we can take ourselves and everyone else around us in a downward spiral. Once we get into that sort of conversation with people everyone in the discussion piles on more and more negativity. We have all either been part of, or at least, heard that sort of conversation. For example one person at work complains about the coffee machine not working, someone else is unhappy about the soap provided in the restroom, someone else has been waiting weeks for a new office chair this all becomes the bosses not caring about the staff, wages are poor and everyone is overworked, underpaid and looking for a new job. Once this conversation has taken place the pile of files on the desk looks twice as high and daunting than it did before.

If we are feeling gratitude for people and/or things around us there is no room for negative emotions and no room for negative thoughts to feed negative emotions.

I really believe that if we feel gratitude we are likely to I feel less pain, less stress and we are less likely to suffer from insomnia. We may find we have stronger immune systems and experience healthier relationships. All of these positive aspects are more prevalent in happy people, gratitude leads to a happier state of mind. So, overall it can boost both our mental health and our physical health.

Gratitude starts with noticing the good things in life. If we have a materialistic outlook and focus and are constantly on wanting possessions to make us happy, we are not likely to be cultivating gratitude because, we are looking at things we don't have not be grateful for what we do have. In other words we are focusing on lack, not on having.

I am not saying that we should not be aspirational, without aspiration we do not have goals to focus on. But I am saying that focusing on lack is not healthy and does not lead to manifesting what we do want. Of course someone who is in dire straits with insufficient food, warmth and shelter is not going to find much to be grateful for.

Equally if we are dependent on another person to make us happy, we are going to struggle with gratitude because we are making our happiness dependent on them being happy rather than on our own happiness.

So how do we move into this place of gratitude? Well, we all find different things to be grateful for. Some people find just being with family and friends, people they love can help them feel more grateful for the love and support they receive and have the opportunity to give.

Some people like journaling and find it helpful to make notes of things that they have gratitude for. Others find it helpful if just before they go to sleep they think of the good things that have happened that day. Or they think of at least 3 things they are grateful for. I personally don't get out of bed until I have thought of at least six things I am grateful for (it can be hard some days to stop at 6). Any Reiki practitioners reading this will know that one of our precepts is *"Just for today I will have gratitude".*

We can use gratitude to turn what might be negative events into positive ones and help ourselves feel happier about life.

One of my favourite books as a child was Pollyanna by the American writer Eleanor Porter. It tells the story of an orphan by the name of Pollyanna who has to go to live with a very strict aunt. Pollyanna plays what she calls the 'Glad Game' as a coping mechanism. For instance when her aunt puts her in a stuffy attic room without carpets or pictures, she exults at the beautiful view from the high window, she says she is glad to have such a wonderful view. When the aunt tries to punish her niece for being late to dinner by sentencing her to a meal of bread and milk in the kitchen with the servant Nancy, Pollyanna thanks her rapturously because she likes bread and milk, and she likes Nancy so much that she is glad that her aunt decides that the meager meal was to be the punishment.

So whether we call it gratitude or call it The Glad Game, it is about being in a mindful space that brings us a feeling of being in peace with life and our surroundings.

I think the simplest way to start to work with gratitude is to just notice the small things in life that bring us joy such as getting a seat on the train or bus in the morning being 'glad' we did not need to stand all the way to work or to the shops, or feeling grateful that we can find a parking space. Noticing the pleasure we feel when we hear the birds singing, having awareness of a beautiful sunset or conscious of a stranger smiling at us. Really connecting with our heartsease and feeling grateful when people do small things for us like holding a door open for us.

How do you feel inside that someone thought to make you that drink or help you carry a heavy bag?

We can say thank you to people, we can say thank you to the little robin in the garden who sings for us. Instead of focusing on big targets that lie somewhere in the future which we believe will make us happy one day. We need to be focusing on and enjoying the here and now. Be aware that we can sometimes glance at something and think to ourselves 'oh that's a sunset' without actually really going inside of ourselves and feeling the joy it brings and being grateful that the sunset exists and we can see it. If we are mindful we are not skating on the surface of life, we are living it fully.

If we practice gratitude and get into feeling the pleasure that comes with true gratitude, then we come back to ourselves instead of focusing on the outside world.

Some people call it mindfulness, basically being present, truly in touch with, conscious of the here and now, living in the moment and enjoying it.

Gratitude is the best attitude.

Love your life

15 THE JOY OF LIFE

I think I have made it clear that I believe an important aspect of living in mindfulness is enjoying life, really living and wringing as much pure joy out of it as we can. Our tiny gurus show this to us when they play happily with their friends. Close to where I live we have a countryside park I often visit with my tiny guru, within the park are treetop walks wooden pathways constructed and secured in nets strung high in massive conifer trees. I love to watch children as they scamper into these magical high-ways (pardon the pun) often followed by adults who look full of trepidation because they have lost the magic of childhood and see nonexistent danger where the children see an opportunity to be full of fun, joy and exploration.

The treetop walks lead to a huge trampoline area which is also several meters high of the ground. The noise level of children laughing and shouting indicates the fun to be had on the trampoline. The children jumping and bouncing around (and the odd adult) are completely absorbed in the business of fun. They are truly merging themselves in the experience of that moment in time. Perfect mindfulness!

I have tried to describe the mindfulness exhibited in the nets and trampoline as an example of how children just know how to do it naturally.

The same principles apply a child riding a bicycle through puddles with legs stuck out to avoid being splashed which of course is futile but seen as great fun.

Or little toddlers joy when they first learn what it is to play on a slide in the playground or little hands catching leaves as they flutter down from the tree in autumn. I remember my tiny guru especially loving trying to catch the seed pods or 'helicopters' falling and swirling from sycamore trees. Watching them twirl down and trying to grasp one before it reached the ground or was taken off again in a gust of wind.

I remember when my nephew was about six years of age, we took a holiday by the seaside in Cornwall. He and I took great delight standing on the beach with no-one else around and yelling at the tops of our voices over the sound of the crashing waves. He would shout very loudly for a few minutes then drop down onto the sand giggling his head off. These simple games are magical for the child as they experience it. Unfortunately many adults loose that sense of fun and magic but it is there waiting for us. I suspect football supporters experience something similar when their team are playing well.

Think about the things that give you joy and do more of it or think about the things that filled you with delight as a child and try doing them again or something similar. I recently listened to a podcast about the health benefits of skipping, just skipping along, not with a skipping rope but skipping along as children sometimes do. Luckily I have a very secluded garden and non of my family was home, so I tried childish skipping, it really was a lot of fun.

When we have a sense of happiness we immerse ourselves more fully in the experience.

Think about a time in the past when you have been in that state of euphoria and then think about what you felt, saw, smelt and heard. You might have vivid recall of colours, textures or sound tones. You will be surprised at what you can recall, really immerse yourself in that feeling.

Let joy in - its fun

❖

16 THE MUNDANE - Opportunity for mindfulness

We can incorporate our mindful practice into the mundane.

We all have those times in our lives when we have to carry tasks or duties that are less than exciting. I would go as far as to say, we all have to do some things we actually dislike and find distasteful. Some of us, have to do things we can view as boring and some things we actually see as stealing our time when we would rather spend time doing something else. Sometimes we have to do things we don't find interesting or stimulating.

However, even the mundane events are just another experience in this human life. il is an experience in a moment of time.

Life is a series of experiences, some more pleasurable than others, some are learning experiences. We can use those mundane times and tasks as practice for mindfulness. To give you an example, I have in the past not enjoyed ironing laundry. I am aware that some people actually enjoy the task of ironing clothes, but, for me it has always just been a means to an end. By which I mean, I get to wear clothes that do not look creased or I can get into a bed where the sheets are not all crumpled up.

Recently I realised that ironing clothes is an excellent opportunity to practice mindfulness. Historically I have tended to watched a video or listened to a radio programme whilst ironing. But, when I reflected on it, I realised. that I can experience all of my senses and practice gratitude at the same time. I have gratitude for the clothes and linen, I have gratitude I live in a place and time where electricity is readily available and I have easy access to water for the steam iron. I can experience awareness of all of my senses except for taste. The feel of the textures of the various textiles as well as the smoothness of the handle of the iron. I can see the patterns of the textiles, I can watch the creases disappear, I can see and hear the steam as it comes out of the iron in gentle shushing sounds, I can experience myself as I handle the iron and the items being ironed as I focus on being aware of my movements as I move through the task of reducing the pile of ironing. The chore becomes a form of mindful meditation. This in turn results in a feeling of peace and calmness.

When we use distraction techniques as I used to, for instance watching a film whilst carrying out mundane tasks such as ironing, we can be missing out on the experience of life. We are on this earth for such a short time (ask any elderly person and they will agree with this) it is a shame to waste time not being present in the moment.

Think about the parts of your life that you think are mundane and boring, consider how you can use the time spent in in the mundane and turn it into a mindfulness experience

Let little things count

17 HEALTH BENEFITS OF MINDFULNESS

If you have read this book thus far, you will hopefully, have started to enjoy some of the health benefits of your mindfulness practice.

The reason I am including this chapter at the end rather than the start of the book is because I wanted you to experience for yourself how mindfulness can enrich your life rather than me setting up your expectations.

I believe that when it comes to healthy living, experience is a fabulous and wise teacher. However, sometimes improvements in our wellbeing can creep up on us without our noticing.

It is a bit like regular exercise, when you first start out on an exercise regimen. For a while you don't notice any difference in how you look and feel, and then one day, you look in the mirror and notice you have regained a waistline again. Or you suddenly notice how much easier you are moving and how well you feel.

I did say at the beginning of this book that mindfulness is not a magic wand but your mindfulness practice will enrich your life and although it cannot cure all ills, you can however, use it to bring peace and connectedness into your life.

The following are some of the benefits you may have already noticed, if not, continue with your practice and see what changes occur in the future.

If we have spent many years not living in the moment, we can have such an ingrained mindset of being in the past or the future that we become totally oblivious to where we are putting our attention.

You may notice that through increasing your mindfulness that you have reduced your stress and anxiety levels. There is a fine line between stress and anxiety. Stress is part of the human condition, it is our body's reaction to an external trigger such as an event that makes us feel nervous, afraid or frustrated.

The types of short-term event that can cause stress might include work pressure. For instance a deadline that has to be met or having an argument with someone in the workplace or maybe due to unseen circumstances meaning you are going to be late for an important meeting.

Feeling stressed is generally a short-term experience unfortunately some people find themselves experiencing stress long-term. Long-term stress inducing triggers can include chronic illness or long term unemployment which might lead to poverty and or divorce proceedings.

Once the triggering situation is passed the stress level usually goes back down to zero. The more we are able to stay in the moment the easier it is to cope with the things that can potentially trigger our stress responses.

Anxiety can be triggered by stress especially when stress is maintained for an ongoing period of time or if the individual experiences a lot of stressful experiences. For example someone who has a job where they lurch from one stressful situation to another.

Anxiety can also occur in people who are unable to identify the main triggers of stress in their lives. Anxiety is often experienced as feelings of worry and unease. Spending time thinking about past experiences which we view as negative can lead to us feeling depressed.

Worrying about events that have not happened, but, we fear might happen, in the future can induce anxiety.

The more we stay in the present moment and become the observer of our emotions the less we are likely to fall into the bog of anxiety.

Research has shown that mindfulness meditation can help to reduce anxiety. When we are free from anxiety we are open to happiness and joy.

One of the effects of living in a mindful manner is reconnection with self.

Modern life can be so hectic that we can become totally task oriented and so locked into our daily activities at work and at home that we loose sight of who we really are. Those of us who spend time on the internet know that we can loose hours in cyberspace and it can be very easy to loose connection with ourself, our environment and everyone around us. By taking the time to reconnect to self, by being present with where we are, and how we feel, brings us into alignment with life and ourselves.

A lot of people notice that after they have been practising mindfulness for some time, that they have an Improved attention span.

By training ourselves to concentrate on our breathing, focusing on our here and now, we improve our ability to sustain attention.

The more enhanced our ability to sustain attention is the more effective we become in whatever endeavours we engage in this includes our mental processing. When our mental processing improves, we feel sharper and more alive.

That sharp alive feeling is what we are aiming for. Really getting every bit of flavour out of the juice of life. In other words feeling alive and well.

That my friends is mindful living.

Love yourself enough ❖

Thank you so much for reading this book. I hope that it has helped to demystify the practice of living a mindful life and that you have found useful tips you can use in your everyday life.

If you have enjoyed my work please consider giving it a rating where you purchased it. And, if you are so inclined a short review would be wonderful. It really helps other likeminded people to find my work.

You may enjoy my book **Do You Want To Be a Healer/Psychic** available on amazon https://www.amazon.co.uk/dp/B0855C1PMC In Do You Want To Be a Healer/Psychic I have woven into the narrative lots of tips and easy to follow practical exercises to help the reader develop their own skills.
There are stories of meeting spirit guides, astral journeying, healing, working with crystals and messages from spirit.

Elizabeth R Gelhard

About the Author

Elizabeth is a clinical hypnotherapist, advanced practitioner in EFT and a Reiki Master.

Validated Practitioner of the General Hypnotherapy Standards Council Registered Practitioner the General Hypnotherapy Register.

Printed in Great Britain
by Amazon